Rethinking Poverty

Catholic Social Tradition

Preface to the Series

In *Tertio millennio adveniente,* Pope John Paul II poses a hard question: "It must be asked how many Christians really know and put into practice the principles of the church's social doctrine." The American Catholic bishops share the pope's concern: "Catholic social teaching is a central and essential element of our faith . . . [and yet] our social heritage is unknown by many Catholics. Sadly, our social doctrine is not shared or taught in a consistent and comprehensive way in too many of our schools." This lack is critical because the "sharing of our social tradition is a defining measure of Catholic education and formation." A United States Catholic Conference task force on social teaching and education noted that within Catholic higher education "there appears to be little consistent attention given to incorporating gospel values and Catholic social teaching into general education courses or into departmental majors."

In response to this problem, the volumes in the Catholic Social Tradition series aspire to impart the best of what this tradition has to offer not only to Catholics but to all who face the social issues of our times. The volumes examine a wide variety of issues and problems within the Catholic social tradition and contemporary society, yet they share several characteristics. They are theologically and philosophically grounded, examining the deep structure of thought in modern culture. They are publicly argued, enhancing dialogue with other religious and nonreligious traditions. They are comprehensively engaged by a wide variety of disciplines such as theology, philosophy, political science, economics, history, law, management, and finance. Finally, they examine how the Catholic social tradition can be integrated on a practical level and embodied in institutions in which people live much of their lives. The Catholic Social Tradition series is about faith in action in daily life, providing ways of thinking and acting to those seeking a more humane world.

Michael J. Naughton
University of St. Thomas
Minnesota, USA

Rethinking Poverty

Income, Assets,
and the Catholic Social Justice Tradition

James P. Bailey

University of Notre Dame Press
Notre Dame, Indiana

Manufactured in the United States of America

Library of Congress Cataloging-in-Publication Data

Bailey, James P. (James Patrick), 1960–
   Rethinking poverty : income, assets, and the Catholic social justice
tradition / James P. Bailey.
        p. cm. — (Catholic social tradition)
   Includes bibliographical references and index.
   ISBN-13: 978-0-268-02223-5 (pbk. : alk. paper)
   ISBN-10: 0-268-02223-2 (pbk. : alk. paper)
   1. Social justice—Religious aspects—Catholic Church.   2. Poverty—
Religious aspects—Catholic Church.   I. Title.
   BX1795.S62B35   2010
   261.8'325—dc22

                                                        2010024326

To the memory

of my parents

Mary Bernadine Bailey

and Timothy C. Bailey

Contents

Acknowledgments   ix

Introduction   1

ONE   Why Asset Building for the Poor?   5

   The Income Paradigm   7
   The Welfare Reform Debate of 1996: An Income-Paradigm
      Debate   9
   The Asset Paradigm   12
   The Role of Current Policy: Exacerbating Wealth
      Inequality   18

TWO   Assets, the Poor, and Catholic Social Teaching   25

   Asset Building for the Poor and Catholic Social Thought   26
   Property and Ownership in Catholic Social Teaching   27
   Contributions of Catholic Social Thought to
      Asset-Building Policy   43
   Contributions of Asset-Building Research to Catholic Social
      Thought   54

THREE   Assets and Human Capabilities   61

   Globalization and the Need for a Cross-Cultural Ethic   64
   Capabilities and Assets   74

FOUR   Asset Discrimination   85

Asset Discrimination in U.S. History 87
The Stubborn Persistence of Asset Discrimination 98
The Cost of Asset Denial 100
Conclusion 102

FIVE   Toward Inclusive Ownership   103

Asset Development for the Poor: Retrieving a Lost
    Tradition 104
Are Asset-Building Proposals Politically Viable? 112
The Promise and Perils of Asset Building for the Poor 114

Appendix:
A Primer on Modern Catholic Social Teaching   127

Notes   132

Bibliography   156

Index   167

Acknowledgments

No book comes into being through the sole efforts of the author and this book is no exception. I am grateful to Duquesne University, especially President Charles Dougherty and Provost Ralph Pearson, for the support and encouragement they have given me throughout this project. Duquesne University has provided significant financial support at various stages in the writing of this book. A Wimmer Family Foundation grant helped support my first scholarly presentation on the subject of asset building at the Annual Meeting of the Society of Christian Ethics. My first published article on asset building, which appeared in the *Journal of the Society of Christian Ethics*, emanated from that lecture. A second Duquesne grant, the Presidential Scholarship, helped fund a presentation I gave at Villanova University on the preferential option for the poor and asset building. That presentation was further developed and published in the *Journal for Catholic Social Thought*. Portions of both articles appear in chapters one and two of this book. I wish to thank as well Duquesne's Center for the Study of Catholic Social Thought for awarding me with a Paluse Fellowship. This fellowship helped to fund the research and writing of the third chapter on capabilities and asset building.

My Departmental Chair at Duquesne, George Worgul, Jr., has been an unwavering supporter throughout the whole book project. He read multiple versions of the manuscript providing helpful and insightful feedback. His unflagging encouragement and tireless advocacy made possible the completion of this book. I am also grateful for the special support and encouragement I have received from two of my departmental colleagues. Gerald Boodoo read the manuscript in its entirety and Dan Scheid read several chapters of the book. Their feedback helped to focus and sharpen the book's argument. I am deeply grateful to them. I also want to acknowledge Mary Filice, a doctoral candidate in the Theology Department at Duquesne, who provided research related to the third chapter of the book.

I have been fortunate as well to be able to avail myself of the expertise and counsel of persons and institutions outside of Duquesne. Lisa Sowle Cahill, the J. Donald Monan Professor of Theology at Boston College, has provided perceptive and insightful feedback at crucial stages during the writing of the book and the final manuscript is much improved as a result. Michael Sherraden, the Benjamin E. Youngdahl Professor of Social Development at Washington University in St. Louis, encouraged me to continue with this project after reading the first article I published on asset building for the poor. Given Sherraden's stature in the field of asset-building research, his demonstration of interest in the book project early on was enormously important. Ray Boshara, Vice President and Senior Research Fellow and former Director of the Asset Building Program at the New America Foundation, has been a constant source of information, encouragement, and inspiration throughout the writing of this project. Elisabeth Brinkmann, R.S.C.J., a friend and colleague for many years, has been reading and correcting drafts of my work for almost as long as I have known her. This manuscript was no exception. The same can be said for my friends Tom Dickens, Joyce Schuld, and Jennifer Wright Knust, accomplished scholars in their own right. They have always found the time to help me throughout this project. I wish also to thank Debi Jo Packer for her encouragement and the uniquely valuable perspective she offered during the writing of this book. Gina Hiatt also provided numerous practical suggestions that helped to advance the book's completion. Special thanks to my editor at the University of Notre Dame Press, Charles Van Hof, who has put up with me missing numerous self-imposed deadlines and has done so with good cheer. He has always given me the time I needed to get my work done while still managing to move the project along with amazing speed when it was necessary to do so. Thanks Chuck. I would also like to thank my copyeditor, Carole Roos, for her thoroughness and keen attention to detail. Her careful reading of the manuscript has greatly improved the final product.

Saving the best for last, I want to thank my wife and best friend Shelley Thacher. It is not always easy to live with someone who teaches and writes for a living but she does so with grace and good humor. It is no exaggeration to say that without her support—emotional, intellectual, and material—this book could not have been written.

Introduction

Economic inequality in the United States has reached its highest level since the beginning of the New Deal, leading a number of scholars and commentators to describe the first decade of the twenty-first century as a "new gilded age."[1] In such an age it is especially appropriate to rethink public policy approaches to poverty, policies that have focused almost exclusively on addressing the income and consumption needs of the poor while neglecting the role that savings and asset building can play in helping the poor to become nonpoor. This focus on income and consumption alone has much to do with the way in which we define poverty, which is almost always *exclusively* in terms of insufficient income. This definition is evident in policies of the political left that attempt to bolster income, like minimum wage laws, and in cash and non-cash income supports, such as food stamps, housing subsidies, earned income tax credits, and private charity. Although those on the political right balk at current levels of government income assistance, expressing concern that such programs create dependencies while devaluing hard work and personal responsibility, they would readily agree with their left-wing rivals that the surest way out of poverty is through increasing income. Poverty as insufficient income is the only way most of us have been trained to conceptualize and to remedy the problem. By contrast, this book rests on the idea that poverty must be conceived more broadly in terms of both insufficient income *and* deficient assets. A robust, effective, and morally adequate response to poverty must go beyond traditional income-enhancement strategies to include complementary efforts aimed at enabling asset development in the poor.

My analysis is interdisciplinary in scope, drawing upon writings from religious, philosophical, and social scientific perspectives. I make use of a significant body of Catholic social teachings that address the problems of poverty. This literature promotes several fundamental principles, virtues, and values I use to underwrite an asset-development approach to reducing poverty. Many Catholic authors also delineate a complex social, political, and cultural definition of poverty that goes beyond simple income calculations, requiring detailed analyses of conditions and structures from different disciplinary and societal perspectives. Given this focus on the conditions and structures of poverty, there has been surprisingly little attention paid by Catholic ethicists to the actual impact on the poor of *public policies* stimulating ownership. A central purpose of this book is to redress this shortcoming, expanding the application of Catholic social justice principles and values to the issue of asset ownership for low-income individuals and households. This critical and constructive use of Catholic social thought is strengthened and complemented by bringing it into conversation with the "capabilities approach" of the philosopher Martha Nussbaum and a growing body of socioeconomic literature and policy analysis aimed explicitly at enabling the poor to acquire and develop assets.

My hope is that this effort to bring these various bodies of work into mutually critical conversation will be helpful to sociologists, economists, political scientists, and policymakers already involved in debates about asset development for the poor, as well as to Catholic social ethicists, for whom this research is largely unknown. In addition, it will be useful to churches and other faith-based programs in their outreach efforts to the poor. The cross-disciplinary conversation of this project also models a much more ambitious goal: to bridge divides between entrenched patterns of public debate and discourse, particularly between those on the political and religious left and right, and to provide common ground where both sides can work together to alleviate poverty.

The first chapter of the book, "Why Asset Building for the Poor?" adumbrates an argument made by the book as a whole, namely, that asset-based approaches to poverty reduction are compatible with religious and non-religious reflection on just economic relationships. It introduces the rationale and benefits of an asset-based approach to poverty alleviation while providing a critical review and analysis of income-based efforts to reduce poverty. The goal of this chapter is threefold: first, to demonstrate the often overlooked qualitative differences between income and wealth, highlighting the distinctive contribution that each makes to the well-being of persons; second, to stress that the pathway out of poverty is not through income and consumption alone, but through savings and investment as well; and third, to illustrate the degree to which the accumulation of financial and other assets is facilitated by institutional structures and public subsidies for the nonpoor and to urge that similar supports should be made available to the poor. If similar subsidies were provided to the poor, public policies would be more equitable and efforts to reduce poverty more effective.

The second chapter, "Assets, the Poor, and Catholic Social Teaching," reviews papal social encyclicals from Leo XIII's *Rerum Novarum* to John Paul II's *Centesimus Annus,* as well as the U.S. Catholic bishops' pastoral letter on the economy, *Economic Justice for All.* The chapter traces the position of Catholic social teaching on the meaning and purpose of ownership and places ownership in relation to central concepts addressed by the tradition including wealth, property, human dignity, and the social nature of the person. This analysis shows that Catholic social teaching shares a great deal with the perspective and approach of social scientists currently working on asset-development strategies for the poor, in particular, recognition of the social nature of the human person and the impact of social and economic structures on individual well-being. The final part of the chapter suggests ways in which the Church's social teaching can contribute to policy discussions regarding asset development for the poor while also articulating what Catholic social teaching can learn from those currently working in the field of asset building.

The third chapter, "Assets and Human Capabilities," draws from the work of the philosopher Martha Nussbaum who argues that current measures of economic analysis rest upon impoverished notions of human well-being and shallow understandings of the moral meaning of income and wealth. Nussbaum's "capabilities approach" stresses that the evaluation of the well-being of a given society must move beyond traditional economic analysis—which tends to associate the idea of consumption with well-being, while also conflating aggregate economic activity with the well-being of particular individuals—toward a consideration of how well that society is promoting the development of human capabilities. Nussbaum's normative evaluation of modern economic arrangements has much in common with Catholic social thought in that both agree that wealth and income are not ends in themselves but are good only insofar as they promote human flourishing and that meaningful work is integral to leading a full human life. Nussbaum's elaboration of what constitutes human flourishing has certain affinities with the Catholic tradition that are due, in part, to their shared appropriation of an Aristotelian heritage. As in the case of Catholic social thought, the capabilities approach has much in common with the thinking of those working in the asset-development field, particularly their understanding of asset building for the poor as integral to the development and exercise of human capabilities.

The fourth chapter, "Asset Discrimination," assesses the differential impact of asset-based policies on two sectors of the population in the United States: white and black Americans. It reviews the social scientific literature and demonstrates that the discrepancies between black and white standards of living cannot be understood without an appreciation of the degree to which blacks have been denied access to benefits that promote and materially reward asset accumulation. I examine the history and long-term impact of such public policies as the Homestead Act, the Social Security Act, the G.I. Bill, and federal home loan programs. This chapter shows that differences in wealth between white and black Americans have been exacerbated by public policies that supported and subsidized asset building for whites while denying the same to blacks. Put more positively, it demonstrates that public policies do matter and must be *inclusive* rather than exclusive.

The final chapter, "Toward Inclusive Ownership," examines policy recommendations and programs proposed and implemented by those working in the asset-development field. These recommendations and programs aim to include *all* Americans in asset-building initiatives. In particular, the chapter looks closely at savings vehicles for the poor known as "individual development accounts" (IDAs) and similar domestic and international initiatives whose purpose is to stimulate asset accumulation for the poor. The chapter then considers criticisms of the asset-building approach to poverty. It argues that Catholic social teaching and the human capabilities approach can help address these criticisms by providing a moral vision to guide the development of asset-building programs and policies in ways that are truly just.

CHAPTER ONE

Why Asset Building for the Poor?

The vision that underlies this proposal [asset building for the poor] is that insofar as possible, each individual should be encouraged to develop to his or her greatest potential, not only as a matter of humanistic values, but as a matter of long term economic competitiveness of the nation, social cohesion, and vitality of our democratic political institutions.

—Michael Sherraden, *Assets and the Poor*

In the early 1930s, the psychologist Norman Maier conducted a series of experiments to develop deeper insight into the human reasoning process and, in particular, into the process of problem solving. One of these experiments

> was carried out in a large room which contained many objects such as poles, ringstands, clamps, pliers, extension cords, tables and chairs. Two cords were hung from the ceiling, and were of such length that they reached the floor. One hung near a wall, the other from the center of the room. The subject was told, "Your problem is to tie the ends of those two strings together." He soon learned that if he held either cord in his hand he could not reach the other. He was then told that he could use or do anything he wished.[1]

All the subjects (University of Chicago faculty, graduate and undergraduate students, both women and men) were able to figure out how to join the two ends of the ropes together using one of several objects in the room. However, only a few people thought to bridge the distance between the two cords by swinging the rope back and forth like a pendulum. For those not able to figure out this more "original" method, Maier provided a subtle hint. Walking around the room, he passed "the cord which hung at the center of the room [putting] it in slight motion a few times." For many subjects, this assistance quickly led to the use of the pendulum approach to solve the problem.[2]

Maier recounts the subjects' own explanations of how they fastened upon the idea of using the pendulum approach to solve the problem with which they were tasked. "Nearly all of the subjects were surprised when asked to tell about their experience of getting the idea of a pendulum and said that they did not think that they could explain it." When pressed they said such things as:

> "It just dawned on me"; "It was the only thing left"; "Perhaps a course in physics suggested it to me"; "I tried to think of a way to get the cord over here, and the only way was to make it swing over." A professor of Psychology reported as follows: "Having exhausted everything else, the next thing was to swing it. I thought of the situation of swinging across a river. I had imagery of monkeys swinging from trees. This imagery appeared simultaneously with the solution. The idea appeared complete."[3]

The reports of the subjects who came up with the pendulum approach only after receiving the hint are "in every respect similar to those" who came up with this approach without receiving the hint. Maier speculates that the subjects did not give any credit to the one who had helped them solve the problem because the subjects did not consciously experience the assistance provided to them by the experimenter. This could have been due to the subtle integration of the assistance into the overall scene. It seems plausible as well that the cultural context in which the experiment took place could have influenced this lack of awareness. In the United States, great rhetorical emphasis is given to the notion of "rugged individualism," an emphasis that obscures the myriad ways lives are sustained by something other than sheer personal effort. Conversely, this same rhetoric tends to stigmatize the need for outside help. For these reasons, even when assistance is provided, it may not be consciously experienced as such.

The subjects in Maier's experiment are illustrative of a dynamic at play on a much wider scale among Americans who have accumulated financial and real assets. Many nonpoor Americans are unaware of the substantial level of institutional and material support that has helped them to save and accumulate assets. This lack of awareness, in turn, leads them to exaggerate their own role in asset accumulation. Of those who hold and accumulate assets, very few realize that they are the beneficiaries of a vast institutional and social network that facilitates and rewards them in ways that contribute significantly to their financial well-being. Just as the assistance that Maier provided to his subjects was so subtle and well integrated into the surroundings as to be outside of their conscious awareness, the systemic assistance provided to help the nonpoor accumulate assets is often so seamlessly integrated into their lives that it is not perceived as such.

Such lack of awareness would not be nearly so problematic if it did not have the potential to influence the judgments many make about the poor and the reasons for their poverty. If people are unaware of the public and private support that contributes to their own ability to save and accumulate assets or, alternatively, if they believe that asset accumulation and asset building are solely the products of their own initiative, sound reasoning, and judgment, they will be far more likely to locate the responsibility for asset poverty with those who are poor. Conversely, raising awareness about the degree to which public and private institutions facilitate savings and asset accumulation for the nonpoor may help to generate support for analogous types of assistance for those who are now poor.

THE INCOME PARADIGM

Most people would agree with Stuart Rutherford's assertion that "a popular and useful definition of a poor person is someone who does not have much money."[4] The development of social policy within modern nation-states, however, requires a more precise definition of poverty, such as a monetary threshold that distinguishes the poor and nonpoor. A more exacting definition of poverty has tended to focus on two primary concepts: consumption and income. Since income as such has no inherent value, economists have looked to the purpose or end of income to generate a more precise understanding of what it means to be poor or nonpoor. In identifying the "end" or "goal" of money, economists necessarily make a judgment of moral value, even though they frequently understand themselves to be engaged in a value-free enterprise. Charles Clark has suggested that for neoclassical economics, the long-standing dominant model within the discipline, the "ultimate good or value in the economy" is "consumption."[5] Thus "human well-being is to be assessed by the availability of disposable income or according to goods consumed; it is measured by the levels of utility achieved in the consumption of commodities."[6] Just as well-being or welfare is defined in relation to consumption, so too is poverty. In keeping with the neoclassical perspective, Oxford's *Dictionary of Economics* defines poverty as the "inability to afford an adequate level of consumption."[7] The so-called "poverty line" marks the point where one has "just enough [income] to avoid inadequate consumption."[8]

From the dominant perspective of neoclassical economics, then, well-being and poverty are intimately linked to income and consumption: the consumption level enabled by one's income determines whether or not one is impoverished. As Michael Sherraden, a leading academic expert on asset-building policy, states:

> Almost entirely, poverty and welfare in Western welfare states have been defined in terms of income. It has been assumed that if households have a certain amount of income, they will consume at a level equivalent to that income, and this consumption is by definition welfare (well-being) of the household. This is consistent with the definition of *welfare* as it is used in welfare economics, and, indeed, the entire edifice of the welfare state rests uneasily on this narrow intellectual footing.[9]

The link between economic poverty, income, and consumption is so pervasive that it is difficult to conceptualize poverty in any other terms. Reflecting this widely accepted perspective (and, no doubt, reinforcing it as well), the federal government defines the official poverty line for individuals and families according to income level, determined by a formula that relies on estimated minimum consumption needs of individuals or families. Established in the mid-1960s the official poverty line was based on a 1955 U.S. Department of Agriculture survey of food consumption which estimated that the average American family of four spent one-third of its after-tax income on food. In defining the poverty line, the lowest priced diet considered adequate (the "Economy Food Plan," later termed the "Thrifty Food Plan") was multiplied by three, and subsequently adjusted for inflation and differing family sizes.[10]

Since poverty is understood as having too little income "to afford an adequate level of consumption," the goal of governmental anti-poverty policies has been dominated by efforts to raise the income or purchasing power of the poor. The aim of these policies is to provide just enough financial assistance to allow the poor to consume at a level that raises them out of poverty. The centrality of income and consumption is visible not only in those initiatives generally associated with the term "welfare," but just as often in efforts to "reform" the welfare system. The last significant public debate about "welfare" in the United States illustrates this emphasis.

THE WELFARE REFORM DEBATE OF 1996:
AN INCOME-PARADIGM DEBATE

The 1996 welfare reform bill known as the Personal Responsibility and Work Opportunity Reconciliation Act (PRWORA) brought an end to the federal government's guarantee of financial assistance to the poor. Debates about PRWORA, both before and after the bill's passage, highlighted areas of sharp disagreement between the political left (or liberals) and right (or conservatives) on how best to deal with poverty in this country. Conservatives criticized the magnitude of governmental expenditures for the poor and questioned whether current welfare policy struck the right balance between "the dual goals of providing a cash safety net for families with children and requiring families to work or look for work."[11] Emphasis on the latter goal (requiring families to work), they argued, would benefit both taxpayers and welfare recipients. In their view, Aid to Families with Dependent Children (AFDC) and other government programs that provided support for the poor had the effect of encouraging childbearing, discouraging marriage, and rewarding those who would not join (or rejoin) the labor market. From this perspective, poverty would be reduced only when public policies stopped encouraging dependency upon government by those living in poverty and, instead, encouraged habits of personal responsibility and industry.

Time-limited benefits and paid work are the keys to achieving these goals and, therefore, the key to reducing poverty. Given the proper motivation, the poor will do what other nonpoor citizens routinely did—enter into the free market, work hard, and take advantage of the many opportunities the market provides.[12]

The data thus far, while still inconclusive, suggest that PRWORA has been more successful at reducing the welfare rolls than it has been at raising household income above the poverty threshold. The passage of PRWORA is correlated with dramatic reductions in welfare caseloads, but the cause and meaning of these reductions is the subject of considerable debate. Among other things, the fact that PRWORA became law during an economic boom has made it difficult to discern whether PRWORA or the robust economy led to a drop in the welfare rolls. For those who left welfare, the economic benefits have not yet lived up to conservatives' expectations. Studies looking at employment patterns of those who have left welfare found that "between one half and three-fourths of parents are employed shortly after leaving the welfare rolls . . . and that as many as 87 percent have been employed at some point" after leaving welfare. However, these same studies show that average reported annual earnings from this employment ranged from "as low as $8,000 to as high as $15,144, leaving many families below the poverty line."[13] The primary reason for the low earnings is stagnant low wages "despite years of work." When earnings do rise, it is primarily because of an increase in work hours rather than wages.[14] As one might expect, these low-wage jobs do not typically include "paid vacations, sick leave, or employer sponsored health insurance."[15] Whatever the virtues of being gainfully employed, work in and of itself does not guarantee a poverty-free life.

The results to date of PRWORA, while not wholly in keeping with the dire predictions of those on the political left, are largely consistent with liberal expectations. Many liberals who opposed PRWORA did not disagree with conservatives that employment should be a key ingredient in the war on poverty. Nor did they disagree with the judgments of conservatives that the welfare system contained many features that have a negative impact on the poor. David Ellwood, for example, acknowledges that the welfare system has undermined work motivation and family stability while contributing to the marginalization of the poor from the rest of society.[16] The opposition to PRWORA by the political left was rooted in the belief that a retreat from federally guaranteed means-tested income transfers would erode some of the most important resources for mitigating the effects on the poor of indifferent, rapidly changing, and sometimes hostile social, political, and economic forces. While recognizing the positive value of work, the political left argued that the dire situation of those in poverty demands government interventions. The suggested interventions typically included a variety of means-tested cash and non-cash income supports and raising the minimum wage.[17]

A great deal of evidence can be adduced in favor of the liberal approach to support for the poor. Government income transfers do, in fact, significantly raise the effective income of the poor, thus easing their burden and substantially increasing the number of persons living above the official poverty line. While the passage of PRWORA did reduce government transfers, for those unable to make up the difference through paid work, the result was a significant drop in their standard of living. For example, "between 1995 and 1997 the poorest single mothers experienced a significant decline in their average disposable incomes, largely owing to sizable decreases [in support] from means-tested programs. . . ."[18] Similarly, a 1998 study looked at the effects of government transfers on income levels of the poor and found that if "government benefits are included in income . . . 6.4 percent of [U.S.] families had annual incomes below $10,000 in 1998. When government benefits are ignored, the fraction with an annual income below $10,000 more than doubles, rising to 14 percent of all families."[19] Clearly, government transfers do significantly increase the levels of disposable income of many poor Americans, thereby reducing some of the hardship associated with poverty.

At the same time, the evidence compiled over a substantial number of years suggests that while income transfers are effective in addressing the *symptoms* of poverty, they appear to be less effective in altering the *underlying causes* that lead to poverty. One piece of evidence supporting this claim is the persistent *pre-transfer* rate of poverty (i.e., the rate of poverty when government transfers are not included). Michael Sherraden has shown that while "official poverty declined from 17.3 percent of the U.S. population in 1965 to 14.4 percent in 1984, pretransfer poverty did not decline—it was 21.3 percent in 1965 and 22.9 percent in 1984." While income transfers have eased the burden of poverty, "they have not helped reduce the underlying level of poverty."[20]

Although the political left and right have different approaches to the problem of poverty, they share the belief at the center of almost all public policy approaches to this problem: that poverty is best understood as a state of deficient *income*. The reason deficient income is impoverishing is that it limits the ability of a person or family to "secure a minimal level of consumption."[21] The focus on income is not unique to liberals or conservatives, it is a belief shared by many, both within and outside public policy circles. When poverty is defined in this way, the prescriptions for overcoming poverty are focused almost entirely on securing a level of consumption at or above the poverty line. Thus, whether it be through means-tested income transfers such as food stamps or rental subsidies, increases in the minimum wage, the earned income tax credit, or even restrictions on benefits to overcome alleged resistance to entrance into the workplace, the goal is almost always related to increasing the income and consumption levels of those who are poor.

The *exclusive* focus on income in public policy approaches to reducing poverty needs to be challenged. The issue is not whether income is important; it clearly is. Rather, the issue is whether income by itself is *sufficient* to give the poor the necessary financial resources to lift them out of poverty. Income-based policies need to be augmented by policies that help the poor to accumulate assets.

THE ASSET PARADIGM

Over the past two decades, a relatively new public policy approach to poverty known as "asset building for the poor" has been the subject of increasingly vigorous debate among social scientists, policy advocates, and politicians.[22] Those working to develop policies that help the poor accumulate assets raise important questions about the adequacy of current definitions of human poverty and human well-being and the policies that flow from these definitions.[23]

Contrary to the notion that poverty and economic well-being ought to be understood solely in terms of income and consumption, advocates of an asset-building approach to poverty argue that income and consumption do not exhaust the meaning of economic poverty. Moreover, they argue that restricting the definition along these lines undermines the effectiveness of anti-poverty initiatives—until such initiatives incorporate some notion of asset building, long-term efforts to alleviate poverty cannot succeed. Economic well-being includes not only adequate income flow and the consumption of goods and services necessary for daily living, but also saving and accumulation of assets, or wealth.[24] Thus, Sherraden argues:

> While income and consumption are obviously important, it is also true that most people cannot spend their way out of poverty. Most people who leave poverty—or to use another vocabulary, most people who develop economically—do so because they save and invest in themselves, in their children, in property, in securities, or in enterprise to improve their circumstances. This being the case, it occurred to me that another way of thinking about the concept of welfare is required, not to replace the income-based definition, but to complement it. This new concept of well-being would focus on asset accumulation.[25]

Sherraden makes it clear in this passage that asset-based approaches are not intended to replace income-based approaches, but rather, to complement them. Income-based strategies to deal with poverty help serve the important function of addressing the immediate needs of those who are poor, and it is important not to misread asset-building policies as representing a replacement for income-based strategies.

To speak of asset building as a "paradigm" is to suggest that the asset-building approach marks a substantial shift in the goals and purpose of public policy for the poor. Most income-based approaches to poverty reduction were (and are) viewed as stopgap measures to help people through a financial crisis brought on by loss of work, unexpected illness, the death of a wage earner, and so on. But poverty remains a persistent problem in the United States (and elsewhere) and one reason for this (although surely not the only reason) is that those living in poverty have not been able to build a secure financial foundation that would help keep them out of poverty. This goal of developing a more permanent and enduring remedy to poverty, backed by a coherent strategy for achieving this goal, distinguishes asset-building approaches from other policy initiatives over the last thirty or forty years.

To see more clearly why asset building for the poor should be integral to efforts aimed at reducing poverty, consider the financial statement of any business. This statement typically includes a summary of revenues and expenses, on the one hand, and assets and liabilities, on the other. Subtracting expenses from revenues gives the total income for that year. Subtracting liabilities from assets yields the total worth of the company's assets (or liabilities). The presence of these two primary categories—income *and* assets—in the financial statement of any business is not accidental. It denotes the existence of two types of financial resources, both *necessary* to the well-being of the business, and both addressing *different* financial needs of the business.

Now consider two businesses, both occupying the same market sector, each with just enough revenues to cover expenses (i.e., income is essentially zero). One of these businesses, Company A, has substantial total assets while the other, Company B, has essentially no assets at all. Now imagine some possible scenarios: a deep and lasting recession; the onset of new technology requiring substantial expenditures for employee training if the business is to keep up with its competitors; the opportunity to purchase the building that houses the business during a time of unprecedented low interest rates; the chance to expand the business by purchasing another company engaged in a complementary enterprise.

In each case, Company A is in a much better position than Company B to deal with the challenges and opportunities presented. The added flexibility provided by Company A's assets would likely enable it to survive in a recession, drawing down its assets when necessary to cover day-to-day expenses. It would also be able to maintain, perhaps even enhance, its competitive position by providing additional training to its employees or through the purchase of a complementary business. Another potential benefit for Company A is the ability to add substantially to its asset base while taking advantage of low interest rates and doing away with non-productive rental payments.

The benefits to Company A go beyond these basic financial advantages, however. One or more of these actions would likely have a positive impact on the attitudes and work performance of the employees, inasmuch as the increased opportunities of the company also provide increased opportunities for the employees. This, in turn, may lead to a more pleasant work environment than would otherwise be the case. Taken together, the opportunities afforded to Company A because of its asset holdings and the positive impact these actions can have on its employees do more than simply keep Company A "afloat." They have the potential to enhance both its income and its assets, placing it on an even better financial foundation.

By contrast, Company B will likely find itself struggling for its very survival during a recession. It may need to lay off a substantial number of employees, thereby depriving itself of one of its most significant non-financial assets—its trained workforce. Undoubtedly these layoffs would depress the morale and enthusiasm of the remaining employees, sapping their motivation to work at Company B. Alternatively, Company B might seek to borrow funds to cover its short-term expenses until the recession passes. Its lack of financial assets, however, will give most loan managers pause. The bank may still decide to fund the loan but, because of the risks involved, the loans will be made at much higher rates than would be available to Company A. Higher interest payments and longer terms will further endanger the day-to-day operations. Business opportunities of the kind that Company A was able to exploit will not be a likely possibility for Company B. At the very least, Company B would be rightfully hesitant to pursue options such as purchasing another company or making a significant capital purchase, since these would only add to its debt burden. More likely, Company B would not even think of doing such things as it would be consumed with the difficulties of simply making ends meet. Going forward, even if day-to-day operating expenses can be met, the condition of Company B is precarious unless and until it can accumulate enough assets to provide some measure of financial security.

By analogy, the above example can serve to illustrate why income alone is not a sufficient strategy for helping the poor to move out of poverty. Assets are not simply a luxury for households but are absolutely essential if they are going to achieve any kind of financial stability. Under normal circumstances, households will use income to secure consumable goods and services, much like businesses use cash flow to cover day-to-day expenses. Like our hypothetical Company A, households with assets will generally be in a better position to deal with unexpected difficulties than households that lack assets. Just as a business with significant assets can withstand economic downturns, so too a household with assets is better positioned to deal with unforeseen or unavoidable events that temporarily curtail or stop income flow—a recession, for example, or a serious illness, the loss of a spouse, or a seriously ill child. At the same time, households with assets will enjoy access to those things that consumption income cannot generally provide, such as a down payment for a home, capital to begin a business, or access to higher education.

The failure to appreciate the very different roles that income and assets play in the household is one reason why public policy has maintained a focus on income. But as this simple exercise shows, income and assets are deployed for very different purposes. Melvin Oliver and Thomas Shapiro underscore the distinction between income and assets (to which they refer as wealth):

> Wealth is a special form of money not used to purchase milk and shoes and other life necessities. More often it is used to create opportunities, secure a desired stature and standard of living, or pass class status on to one's children. In this sense the command over resources that wealth entails is more encompassing than is income or education and closer in meaning and theoretical significance to our traditional notions of economic well-being and access to life's chances.[26]

Oliver and Shapiro's observation regarding the qualitatively distinct goods secured by assets versus income alone is confirmed by studies documenting the distinctive psychosocial effects of the benefits associated with assets on individuals and families who hold them. After an extensive review of published research examining the effect of asset ownership on neighborhoods, families, and children, Edward Scanlon and Deborah Page-Adams concluded that there was growing evidence that assets "are associated with economic household stability; decrease economic strain on households; are associated with educational attainment; decrease marital dissolution; decrease the risk of intergenerational poverty transmission; increase health and satisfaction among adults; decrease residential mobility; increase property maintenance; [and] increase local civic involvement."[27] Michael Sherraden has also looked at the psychosocial effects of assets and suggested that, in addition to the effects noted by Scanlon and Page-Adams, assets create long-term thinking and planning, provide a foundation for taking risk, increase personal efficacy and sense of well-being, lead to greater development of human capital, increase social status and social connectedness, and enhance the well-being and life chances of offspring.[28]

By contrast, households that do not have any substantial assets will face greater and more frequent difficulties and obstacles than those with assets. Like Company B in the example above, households without assets will be far less able to deal with unexpected interruptions in income flow: recessions will hit these households harder; family deaths or illnesses will be much more likely to cause serious economic distress. The lack of a financial cushion helps to explain why welfare recipients move in and out of the welfare system, usually staying on the welfare rolls for relatively brief periods. Loss of income, in the absence of asset ownership, can be disastrous, leaving those who are poor with no other recourse but governmental or other charitable aid to make up for income shortfalls. Even when things are going as they should, the stress and strain of making ends meet will take its toll. Moreover, the demands and pressures of meeting day-to-day expenses and of trying to forestall economic disaster will often crowd out considerations of future possibilities.

In her powerful memoir *Unafraid of the Dark*, Rosemary Bray vividly describes the anxiety, tension, and energy-sapping existence that the poor face on a daily basis:

> One of the truths that seem to elude most welfare reformers is the pervasive sense of fear and tension that accompanies that monthly [welfare] check. I learned to decipher that look of tension in my mother's eyes: it's the fear of knowing that the best you can do is to give a little something to everyone you owe. Not enough to pay them, sometimes not enough to placate them, but just enough to remind them—and you—that you can never really catch up. . . . There is no money to plan ahead, to shop cheaply, to prepare for an emergency. There is no ability to set aside a bit for the future; the present occupies all the attention of anyone on welfare. Our contingency fund was the streets and alleys, where we searched for bottles we could turn in for the deposits. . . . Sometimes the fear is a matter of timing. Late mail, a bureaucratic mix-up, and a carefully planned method of survival lies in tatters. One month, in the dead of winter, the check was late and every bill in the house was due; some were overdue. When the gas man came to turn off the gas, my mother went outside to meet him, but for once her considerable charm failed her. . . . I can only imagine what went through my mother's

mind as the man left. Surrounded by four hungry children under the age of seven, living in an apartment without cooking gas. . . .[29]

The negative effects of being asset poor fall especially hard on those who are income poor. With no serious possibility of accumulating assets and with few good options by which to raise their income, it is not irrational to become discouraged about future possibilities. Whatever the virtues of income strategies for reducing poverty, they simply do not adequately address the difficulties and precariousness that the poor experience because of their lack of assets. Nor do these strategies create a realistic foundation from which the poor might gain a permanent foothold outside of poverty. For this to happen, an asset-development strategy is needed.

THE ROLE OF CURRENT POLICY:
EXACERBATING WEALTH INEQUALITY

The United States already has in place a variety of initiatives that, taken together, constitute a vigorous and broad-based asset-building policy. The problem is that the beneficiaries of these policies are almost exclusively the nonpoor. Indeed, the current asset-based initiatives are so focused on the nonpoor that it would be accurate to characterize them as a "preferential option for the nonpoor."[30] These policies are biased toward the nonpoor primarily because they deliver subsidies aimed at facilitating savings, ownership, and asset accumulation through the income tax code.

The majority of these asset-building policies give tax deductions for certain types of asset-building endeavors. These deductions are technically referred to as tax expenditures, defined as "revenue losses attributable to provisions of the Federal tax laws which allow a special exclusion, exemption, or deduction from gross income or which provide a special credit, a preferential rate of tax, or a deferral of tax liability."[31] More colloquially tax expenditures are often referred to as tax "loopholes." From a budgetary standpoint, tax expenditures and direct expenditures such as Social Security payments, student financial assistance, unemployment compensation, Medicare, and Medicaid are functionally the same: both cost the government money.[32] A dramatic illustration of how much these expenditures cost the government in lost revenues can be seen by projecting how much lower tax rates would be if tax expenditures were eliminated. According to one calculation, eliminating tax expenditures would "finance a 44 percent across the board reduction of income tax rates (with no AMT [alternative minimum tax]). That would constitute a cut in the top marginal income tax rate from 35 percent to less than 20 percent with no revenue loss."[33]

Both from the perspective of the federal budget and from the perspective of their beneficiaries, policies that subsidize asset building through the tax code are not revenue neutral. The beneficiaries of these policies are provided with significant financial rewards via preferential tax treatment of their asset holdings and the federal government incurs substantial losses of revenue as a result of these same policies. How substantial are these losses of revenue? According to one study, non-business "individual income tax expenditures reduced 2007 federal income tax revenues by as much as $761 billion."[34] This number exceeds the amount of money included in the Troubled Asset Relief Program (TARP) legislation recently passed by Congress, is greater than the 2008 federal budget deficit ($638 billion),[35] is more than the total amount of U.S. defense spending in fiscal year 2008 ($599 billion),[36] is greater than 2008 nondefense discretionary spending ($521 billion),[37] and is roughly fourteen times the size of 2006 direct expenditures of governmental programs that most persons associate with "welfare."[38] From almost any perspective, tax expenditures represent "a massive commitment of fiscal resources."[39] The magnitude of these expenditures leads Christopher Howard to suggest that "the IRS, rather than Health and Human Services, [is arguably] the most comprehensive social welfare agency in the United States."[40]

Nearly all tax expenditures are directed to the nonpoor.[41] Those whose income is $50,000 or more receive approximately 90 percent of the benefit of tax expenditures on home mortgage interest and state and local taxes on income and property, marking these expenditures as the most regressive tax policy in the federal budget.[42] Specific examples of tax expenditures underscore the regressive nature of the asset subsidies provided by the federal government: in 1998, 54 percent of the $47 billion federal expenditure for mortgage interest deductions went to homeowners with annual incomes over $100,000 and 91 percent went to homeowners with incomes over $50,000. Similarly, in 1999, 67 percent of the federal tax expenditure for retirement benefits went to households earning more than $100,000, with 93 percent of the benefits going to those making over $50,000 per year.[43]

Since 1999, the data shows that the regressive nature of the distribution of these benefits has continued unabated. Thus, for example, a 2007 report commissioned by the Federal Reserve Bank (using 2005 data) noted that 45 percent of the benefit of the three largest asset-building policies—preferential treatment of capital gains, mortgage interest deductions, and property tax deductions—go to families whose average annual income exceeds $1 million. By contrast, the lowest 60 percent of households received about 3 percent of the benefits.[44] In terms of the dollar value of the benefit received, "the poorest fifth of Americans get, on average, $3 in benefits from these policies, while the wealthiest one percent enjoy, on average, $57,573. Households with incomes of $1 million or more receive an average benefit of $169,150." Lillian Woo and David Buchholz add:

> By any measure, [the distribution of] these benefits are skewed. Households that earn less than $17,000 receive, on average, $3 in benefits. Perhaps more startling is that households with incomes below $80,000 receive average benefits of less than $1,000 from these policies. At low levels of income, benefits from tax-based asset incentives are small. Increased income brings increases in benefits, though the amount of benefits may not induce a change in asset-building behavior. For example, a family that earns between $30,000 and $35,000 has an average asset subsidy of $74. The pattern of benefits resembles an exponential function with small changes at low income levels growing faster and faster as income continues to rise.[45]

See figure 1 for a graph of the average asset-building subsidies by income. Given this data, it is hard not to agree with Michael Sherraden's conclusion that "public policies for asset building are making the comfortable more comfortable, the rich richer, and leaving the poor as they are."[46]

Another feature of tax expenditures is that they are asset based, "that is, these . . . benefits *directly help people accumulate financial and real assets*."[47] The largest tax subsidies that encourage asset accumulation are in the areas of preferential treatment of gains from investments, retirement accounts, and home ownership.[48] The housing tax expendi-

Figure 1. Average Asset-Building Subsidy

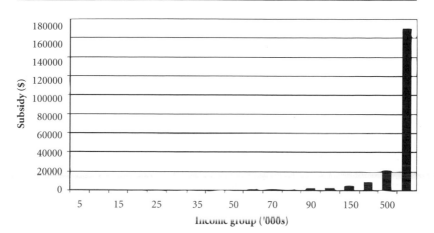

Source: Lillian Woo and David Buchholz, *Subsidies for Assets: A New Look at the Federal Budget, Federal Reserve System* (Washington, DC: Corporation for Enterprise Development, 2007), 10.

ture provides an especially striking example of how these public policies focus on consumption alone for the poor while enabling asset accumulation for the nonpoor. Whereas the nonpoor receive substantial housing subsidies directed at helping them to become *homeowners*, the vast majority of the housing subsidies directed to the poor enable them to secure *rental housing*. Moreover, as Howard points out, the sheer size of the housing tax subsidy for the nonpoor—twice the size of "all traditional housing programs, including Section 8 and rental vouchers and public housing . . . undercuts the prevailing image of 'subsidized housing' as housing for the poor."[49] Howard's point brings to mind a remark made by Michael Harrington that, in the United States, we have "socialism for the rich and free enterprise for the poor."[50]

Tax expenditures share important characteristics with a type of direct expenditure sometimes referred to as "spending entitlements." Perhaps most well known of these spending entitlements are Social Security and Medicare. Howard Shuman provides a colorful illustration of the budgetary similarities between tax expenditures and spending entitlements.

Tax expenditures and spending entitlements are a common breed. They are like the animals in Noah's Ark which marched aboard side by side. Both are automatic and paid out by law and formula. Neither is regularly reviewed. Both are uncontrollable without a change in law. Once legislated, they create powerful interest groups that are dependent on their benefits, deeply entrenched and difficult, if not impossible, to oppose. Tax expenditures and spending entitlements are entered on opposite sides of the budget ledger. While they may not be of the same gender they are of the same species.[51]

Finally, the high level of participation among those who can take advantage of these asset-savings vehicles is directly related to their ease of access and the incentives that they provide. This observation challenges the long-dominant model of saving put forward by neoclassical economists. According to this model, a person's saving habits can be explained in terms of preferences for current or future consumption. Michael Sherraden and Sondra Beverly argue, however, that this widely accepted explanation of savings behavior is inadequate because it fails to take account of the social and institutional context of savings behavior. To fully appreciate why and how people save, one must recognize that savings behavior, like any human behavior, is profoundly influenced and shaped by social and institutional forces. When one examines the context within which saving takes place, it is apparent that there are great differences in the social and institutional settings within which the nonpoor and the poor make decisions about saving.[52]

One of the important differences between the context in which the nonpoor and poor save has already been noticed: the federal government provides the former with significant incentives to save in the form of tax subsidies while there are no such equivalent subsidies available to the poor. But there are other significant differences between the contexts of the nonpoor and poor that influence savings behavior. While the nonpoor have easy access to institutions that facilitate saving, "low-income households frequently have very limited access to these institutions." For example, members of low-income households are "less likely to be in employment situations that offer retirement plans." If they live in low-income neighborhoods, especially low-income minority neighborhoods, they will have less access to local bank branches than members of nonpoor households. In addition, it is "likely that financial sophistication varies by socioeconomic status" implying differential access to financial information and education.[53] Low-income households will also be far less likely to have access to savings incentives: they receive far less benefit from tax deductions for mortgage interest; they generally receive lower rates of return for housing investments; and they rarely have access to employer-matched pension programs. In terms of institutional facilitation of saving, the poor generally cannot save through payroll deductions, mortgage-financed home purchases, and other mechanisms to which the nonpoor have relatively easy access.[54]

In other words, the argument of neoclassical economists that the nonpoor accumulate assets only because they delay present consumption—an argument that contains an unstated but thinly veiled accusation that those who lack assets are simply spendthrifts—ignores the substantial and pervasive social and institutional supports that are in place to help the nonpoor save. As an example, Sherraden notes that the nonpoor "participate in retirement pension systems because it is easy and attractive to do so. This is not a matter of making superior choices. Instead, a priori choices are made by social policy, and individuals walk into the pattern that has been established."[55]

To illustrate: my employer *requires* me to contribute to one of a number of 401(k) savings plans that have been set up for me by the university. The university then matches these savings and makes an additional contribution over and above the match. The tax liability for my and the university's contribution is deferred until I withdraw the money. In the meantime, I do not pay taxes on any of the earnings this money generates until I withdraw it. All of this happens automatically, *before* I receive my paycheck—frugality and wise spending never even enter into the picture in determining what gets saved. Equally important, my employer provides access to a myriad of financial investment options administered by private-sector investment firms. These firms provide, among other things, personal financial advice, including investment advice, access to investment funds of several different varieties, and retirement planning. Again, all of this is facilitated through my employer. Obviously, not all middle- or upper-class persons are provided with matched savings accounts or access to investment services through their employer, but they are far more likely to be provided with these things than those working jobs at lower incomes.

A priori social policies also shape the choices available to the poor, but these policies generally do not have the effect of facilitating saving, let alone providing incentives to do so. Indeed, the main federal social welfare institution to which the poor have access actually *discourages* saving: means-tested welfare benefits set asset limits above which benefits are denied. The idea that the poor are unable to accumulate assets either because they do not make enough money to do so or because of profligate spending habits derives in part from the widely held view that "individuals save as autonomous actors in an unstructured socioeconomic world."[56] This is decidedly not the case. An important question is whether the poor could save if public policies not only refrained from discouraging saving but also provided incentives and institutional support similar to those routinely available to the nonpoor. That question will be taken up in detail in chapter five.

CHAPTER TWO

Assets, the Poor,
and Catholic Social Teaching

Basic justice calls for more than providing help to the poor and other vulnerable members of society. It recognizes the priority of policies and programs that support family life and enhance economic participation through employment and widespread ownership of property.
—National Conference of Catholic Bishops, *Economic Justice for All*

The discussion in chapter one relied on psychosocial scientific arguments about the effectiveness of asset-based strategies. A moral basis for such policies was assumed but never fully developed. For some, this is how it should be, particularly in a pluralistic society such as the United States. Some would even argue that public policy ought to remain neutral vis-à-vis any particular religious or philosophical conception of the good life. For others, particularly those who hold strong commitments to a particular faith tradition or philosophical conception of the good life, it is important that public policy be consistent with these deeply held beliefs.

It is increasingly clear that *any* public policy endorses *some* conception of the human good. The conception of the good that a particular policy endorses may or may not be made explicit, may or may not be coherent, may or may not be appropriate to the society to which the policy applies.[1] Nevertheless, *some* conception of the good informs *all* public policy. The question for any policy, including one aimed at reducing poverty, is not "Shall discussions of policy be value based?" but rather, "Which values shall matter, and how?"[2] Unless one believes that the answer to this question is purely arbitrary, one has a responsibility to construct a reasonable case for the values one defends and to articulate how these values should shape public policy. Additionally, significant public policy innovations are rarely implemented simply on the basis of sound social policy research. More often than not, successful legislative action depends upon whether or not the public finds the moral argument for such policies persuasive.

For these reasons, it is important that those who find the case for asset building for the poor persuasive situate such policies within a moral framework. In this chapter and the next, I situate asset-building policy within the moral perspective of one distinctive religious tradition and one distinctive philosophical perspective in the hope that initiating a moral argument for these policies will begin a wider discussion in which those working in (or at least familiar with) other traditions will find reasons to engage.

ASSET BUILDING FOR THE POOR AND CATHOLIC SOCIAL THOUGHT

One of the strengths of the Catholic social tradition is its development of extended public arguments in support of its position on the economy and other social and political matters.[3] This characteristic, together with its insistence that personal and social well-being would be enhanced if ownership were expanded to include those who possessed little or nothing in the way of real or financial assets, makes it an especially appealing dialogue partner. The link between reducing poverty and expanding ownership to the poor has been present in Catholic social teaching since the publication in 1891 of the very first papal social encyclical, Leo XIII's *Rerum Novarum*.[4] As the tradition developed, its teaching on ownership was accompanied by a developing awareness of the role that social and institutional structures play in facilitating or impeding economic well-being. For this reason it is somewhat surprising that the social scientific literature on asset building for the poor and related policy initiatives have been overlooked in official Church documents and the writings of Catholic social ethicists.

To see how this more recent literature on asset building is relevant to Catholic social thought, it will be helpful first to recall what the tradition has said about ownership and then indicate how this substantive position is related to more general principles and themes. Attending to both the "what" and the "why" of the Church's position on private property will demonstrate how much the tradition shares with the goals of those currently working to create ownership possibilities for the poor.

PROPERTY AND OWNERSHIP IN CATHOLIC SOCIAL TEACHING

Leo XIII. Stressing the Virtues of Ownership

From Leo XIII to John Paul II, the papal social tradition has defended the right of private property and the need to expand private ownership to as many persons as possible. *Rerum Novarum* (1891), the very first social encyclical, written in the context of the industrial era with an eye toward the problems of socialism, sets the direction of the tradition on the question of ownership: "The law . . . should favor ownership, and its policy should be to induce as many as possible of the people to become owners."[5] Like contemporary advocates of asset building for the poor, private ownership has been understood in the Catholic social tradition as a *means to reducing poverty* and inequality. As Leo puts it: "If working people can be encouraged to look forward to obtaining a share in the land, the consequence will be that the gulf between vast wealth and sheer poverty will be bridged over, and the respective classes will be brought nearer to one another."[6] In this context, "nearer" has both a psychosocial and a socioeconomic meaning. Leo was clearly concerned about social unrest and class conflict caused by excessive inequalities and he believed increasing the number of people who owned private property would reduce this tension. The second meaning is implied by the first: social tension and class conflict would be reduced when wealth (and income) inequality were reduced. Thus, persons would be "nearer" to one another economically as well. Leo's endorsement of the right of private ownership is not an endorsement to amass excessive wealth.

Rather, throughout the tradition there is a consistent concern to decrease inequality by spreading ownership to all.

Leo puts forward several arguments in support of private ownership. First, an important reason for engaging in work is to receive remuneration that is sufficiently high for the worker to secure not only an adequate level of goods necessary for day-to-day living but also ownership of property or other assets: "The very reason and motive of... work is to obtain property, and to hold it as his own private possession."[7] If the prudent and relatively frugal worker is not able to secure ownership from paid wages, this is itself *prima facie* evidence that workers' wages are too low.[8] For Leo, working for wages that provide insufficient income to purchase property is equivalent to slavery.[9] Subsequent papal encyclicals will underscore this linkage among work, wages, and ownership.

Second, Leo asserted that private property is part of the natural law and therefore it is a "natural right."[10] As Leo put it, "every man has by nature the right to possess property as his own."[11] *Rerum Novarum* understands private property as a natural right in several ways. It is natural in the sense that God has created the earth for all to use and enjoy and private ownership helps to facilitate this. In addition, since ownership is understood as necessary for meeting the needs of persons, they have a right to private property. Leo sees private property as helping to meet not only immediate needs but future needs as well. This latter quality of private ownership is important because it addresses a particular feature of human nature: the capacity for future-oriented thinking. Private ownership contributes to this mode of thinking by providing the economic stability that facilitates planning for future goals. "[I]t must be within his right to have things not merely for temporary and momentary use, as other living beings have them, but in stable and permanent possession; he must have not only things which perish in the using, but also those which, though used, remain for use in the future."[12] Related to this, Leo recognized that the promise of ownership would give persons hope in their future, particularly for bettering their condition in life.[13] Finally, Leo noticed that an important aspect of private property is that it allows one to transfer wealth to one's children, thereby providing an additional avenue for the care of one's offspring.[14]

While Leo sees private ownership as natural, this does not mean that human institutions do not and should not play a role in assisting persons to become owners. He gives the state a prominent role in facilitating widespread access to ownership. The laws and institutions of the state should be "such as to produce of themselves public well-being and private prosperity."[15] The ultimate goal of the state is to make "the citizens better and happier," and Leo sees private ownership as integral to this goal.[16] While recognizing that employers have a duty to promote the well-being of their workers and that employees have a responsibility to carry out the tasks for which they are employed, Leo insists that the state has a special obligation to protect and promote the well-being of the poor including the working class:

> The richer population have many ways of protecting themselves, and stand less in need of help from the State; those who are badly off have no resources of their own to fall back upon, and must chiefly rely upon the assistance of the State. And it is for this reason that wage earners, who are, undoubtedly, among the weak and the necessitous, should be specially cared for and protected by the commonwealth.[17]

At the same time, Leo recognizes that excessive concentration of wealth and ownership distort the balance of power in society, undermining the power of the state to carry out its rightful duty to promote the common good while providing care and protection for wage earners and their families. The effects of this imbalance of power are not hard to see: easy exploitation of workers, undermining of productive business activity, corruption of the political sphere, and social unrest among the population as a whole. In this way, vast inequalities in wealth undermine the common good, diminishing the quality of life for everyone. Thus the right of property ownership is not without conditions. It has inherent responsibilities and limits that are rooted in the very nature of created goods. In *Rerum Novarum* and the subsequent tradition of Catholic social thought, this twofold affirmation of the right of private property and the responsibilities that come with it are grounded in the doctrine of creation. As Andrew Lustig puts it in his analysis of the papal tradition on private property: "The absolute dominion of God is the basis for claims to, and limitations upon, individual acquisition and possession of property."[18]

Leo stresses that both the state's and employers' obligation to those in need is grounded in the inherent limitations of private property as a created good for all. Furthermore, this obligation is a matter of distributive justice. This is so because "it is only by the labor of the workingman that States grow rich."[19] It follows that it is just that laborers and their families share in the distribution of social goods. While there is a role for almsgiving in any society, fair distribution of wages is not to be understood as an act of charity but, rather, as a demand of justice. When workers are justly treated and justly paid and thereby enabled to become property owners, Leo believed they would work harder and this would add to the wealth of the entire community. Everyone benefits. In a rightly ordered society—one ordered so that the goods of society are justly distributed—there will be less need for charitable poverty relief.[20] In this way, the state's promotion of adequate wages and facilitation of ownership is one way of fulfilling "the province of the commonwealth to consult for the common good."[21]

Several important themes in *Rerum Novarum* will recur again and again in papal social encyclicals as well as resonate with the rationale for asset-building strategies proposed by social scientists and policy analysts working outside of this tradition. Leo recognizes that ownership provides benefits that are qualitatively different from wages alone. These benefits include the possibility of long-range planning thus addressing the capacity and need of human beings to plan for the future. Like today's asset-building advocates, Leo acknowledges that property and other assets are distinctive from income in that, unlike income, they can be transmitted to progeny to enhance their future well-being. He also recognizes that even the possibility of ownership has important effects inasmuch as it offers the hope for improving one's condition in life. Finally, Leo insists that ownership not only has benefits but carries with it responsibilities as well.[22] As we will see, many of these same claims about ownership are also made by social scientists and policy analysts working on ways to expand ownership to the poor.

Pius XI: Developing Leo's Social Teaching

Forty years after *Rerum Novarum,* in the midst of a worldwide economic depression, Pius XI issued *Quadragesimo Anno.* If the primary concern of Leo was that of socialism and the grinding working conditions of the industrial era, Pius XI's principle worry was the excesses of free-market capitalism and the extreme inequalities and patterns of domination it produced. For Pius XI and the Catholic social tradition, the problem with these patterns is that they deny "the legitimate needs which persons have for material well-being of a certain minimum level or for the economic stability which is a psychological necessity of humane existence."[23] More fundamentally, Pius XI points to the tendency of the economic practices of the time to treat some people solely as a means to an end. Accordingly, while he shares his predecessor's negative view of Marxism and socialism, he adopts a much more critical stance toward capitalism.

Like Leo, Pius XI affirms that private property is consistent with the natural law and that ownership implies both individual and social rights and responsibilities. He insists on the individual right to own private property as a means of fulfilling one's responsibilities to provide for oneself and one's family. However, as in Leo, this right is not absolute since the Creator has intended the fruits of creation for all.[24] Private ownership involves public responsibilities. While the state cannot abolish the institution of private property, its social function means that civil authority may appropriately adjust "ownership to meet the needs of the public good."[25] Against those arguing that the state has no right to redistribute or limit private ownership of property, Pius XI asserted that the latter action mitigates against social conflict and helps strengthen the institution of private ownership itself. He states that

> when civil authority adjusts ownership to meet the needs of the public good it acts not as an enemy, but as the friend of private owners; for thus it effectively prevents the possession of private property, intended by nature's Author in his wisdom for the sustaining of human life, from creating intolerable burden and so rushing to its own destruction.[26]

Like Leo, Pius XI recognized that ownership is a key component of economic security and that those who are not yet owners need to be enabled to become so. He recognized that expanding ownership to the working class would not occur "unless the propertyless wage earner be placed in such circumstances that by skill and thrift he can acquire a certain moderate ownership."[27] One "circumstance" that workers need to be "placed in" is a job that pays a living wage, that is, one that will enable ownership through a wage "sufficient for the support of himself and of his family."[28] "But how can he [the laborer] ever save money, except from his wages and by living sparingly, who has nothing but his labor by which to obtain food and the necessities of life?" In the pope's view, supporting oneself and one's family includes saving money and so wages ought to be high enough to enable the worker who lives "sparingly" to do so.[29]

Wages are not the only means through which Pius XI believed workers could and should become owners. Wealth "must be so distributed among the various individuals and classes of society that the common good of all" is promoted. Invoking "social justice"—a phrase for which this pope is rightly remembered—he argues that the "principles of social justice" dictate that "one class is forbidden to exclude the other from a share in the profits."[30] In words that have considerable resonance in the current moment, he chastises "an irresponsible wealthy class who, in their good fortune, deem it a just state of things that they should receive everything and the laborer nothing."[31]

To deal with the problem of extreme wealth inequality and to expand the number of persons who become owners, Pius XI puts forward a proposal that anticipates what would later become an effective wealth-building mechanism for some workers in the decades that followed. He urges that, whenever possible, employees be given part ownership of the company for which they work. In his view, wage contracts should "be modified . . . by a contract of partnership" so that "workers and executives become sharers in the ownership or management, or else participate in some way in the profits" of the company for which they work.[32] In arguing for partnerships, Pius XI tacitly acknowledges that wages alone will not always be sufficient to secure ownership. In advocating for sharing the profits of labor, Pius XI highlights the interdependence of laborer and employer. He notes that when a person works on another's property "the labor of one person and the property of another must be associated, for neither can produce anything without the other." Thus it is "entirely false to ascribe the results of their combined efforts to either party alone; and it is flagrantly unjust that either should deny the efficacy of the other and seize all the profits."[33]

Pius XI evinces acute concern for the problems associated with inequality and the accumulation of wealth in the hands of the few. He finds evidence for an unjust and inequitable distribution of earthly goods in "the immense number of propertyless wage earners on the one hand, and the superabundant riches of the fortunate few on the other."[34] He rejects the idea that "economic affairs . . . be left to the free play of rugged competition" for such an arrangement is bound to favor those who are already in an economically privileged position while doing nothing to address the needs of the poor.[35] Recognizing the power of social and institutional arrangements and the effect that they can have on the most vulnerable in society, Pius XI stresses even more than Leo that extreme inequalities can only be addressed by state intervention. Establishing minimum wages and facilitating employer-employee partnerships are two institutional changes aimed at mitigating inequality. This effort must also go beyond such measures, involving all levels of society—the laborer, the employer/owner, and the state—in a commitment to social justice that enables the worker to participate in the fruits of ownership and thereby securing a stake in the future:

> Therefore, with all our strength and effort we must strive that at least in the future the abundant fruits of production will accrue equitably to those who are rich and will be distributed in ample sufficiency among the workers—not that these may become remiss in work, for man is born to labor as the bird to fly—but that they may increase their property by thrift, that they may bear, by wise management of this increase in property, the burdens of family life with greater ease and security, and that, emerging from the insecure lot in life in whose uncertainties non-owning workers are cast, they may be able not only to endure the vicissitudes of earthly existence but have also assurance that when their lives are ended they will provide in some measure for those they leave after them.[36]

John XXIII and Paul VI: Developing a Global Vision

The period in which John XXIII (1958–1963) served as pope was characterized by a rapid increase in the use of technology, an expansion of governmental institutions, programs, and services, and increased complexity and interdependence of social arrangements. He noted that "one of the principal characteristics of our time is the multiplication of social relationships, that is, a daily more complex interdependence of citizens. . . ."[37] For example, government insurance programs like Social Security were playing an increasingly important role in providing people financial security. These programs are dependent upon the ability of persons to contribute to them, and their ability to do this is dependent upon macroeconomic conditions influenced by both local and international economic activity. Where at one time, for better or worse, a person's retirement security was affected by a relatively circumscribed and straightforward set of conditions, it is increasingly determined by a wide range of social and institutional relationships—local, national, and international.

These and other changes have influenced the meaning, purpose, and value given to property, income, and work. A social system designed to provide persons with long-term security plays a role previously held by private property. The value given to earned income changes and, concomitantly, there is a greater appreciation of work as intrinsically valuable and meaningful. These and other factors raised questions about the relevance of previous papal teachings on ownership. John XXIII answered these questions in the affirmative:

> For the right of private property . . . is permanently valid. Indeed, it is rooted in the very nature of things, whereby we learn that individual men are prior to civil society, and hence, that civil society is to be directed toward man as its end. Indeed, the right of private individuals to act freely in economic affairs is recognized in vain, unless they are at the same time given an opportunity of freely selecting and using things necessary for the exercise of this right. Moreover, experience and history testify that where political regimes do not allow to private individuals the possession also of productive goods, the exercise of human liberty is violated or completely destroyed in matters of primary importance. Thus it becomes clear that in the right of property, the exercise of liberty finds both a safeguard and a stimulus.[38]

While affirming the right of private property, John's commitment to the dignity and equality of all persons leads him to say that "it is not enough to assert that the right to own private property and the means of production is inherent in human nature. We must also insist on the extension of this right in practice to all classes of citizens."[39] Indeed, the very measure of a nation's economic prosperity "is not so much its total assets in terms of wealth and property, as the equitable division and distribution of this wealth." Social progress is equated with a reduction in "social inequalities." The equitable division and distribution of wealth is what "guarantees the personal development of the members of society, which is the true goal of a nation's economy."[40] Like previous popes, John XXIII sees increased wages as one of the major pathways toward expanding ownership, thus enabling "workers to save more readily and hence to achieve some property status of their own."[41] For this pope as well, adequate levels of wages are not a matter of charity but of justice. Remuneration for work should, as a matter of justice and equity, be sufficient to "give the worker and his family a standard of living in keeping with the dignity of the human person."[42] Workers' wages should be "increased within limits allowed by the common good."[43] In addition, like Pius XI, John endorses the idea that workers be given a greater role in companies in which they are employed, including partial ownership of these companies.[44]

John XXIII's successor, Paul VI (1963–1978), more than any previous pope stresses that "private property does not constitute for anyone an absolute and unconditioned right."[45] In particular, "the right to property must never be exercised to the detriment of the common good."[46] While Paul VI recognized that industrialization had made important contributions to the well-being of persons and societies, he railed against a kind of egoistic and extreme individualism that asserted "profit as the key motive for economic progress, competition as the supreme law of economics, and private ownership of the means of production as an absolute right that has no limits and carries no corresponding social obligation."[47] This perspective on economic matters is equated with dictatorship and exploitation. Paul VI emphasizes that persons are not free to accumulate wealth far in excess of their needs. A primary purpose of the institution of private property is to make possible an adequate level of resources for all persons. He insists that the right of property is limited precisely because God intended the goods of the created order for everyone.[48]

Paul's concern about excessive concentrations of wealth on the one hand and an abundance of need on the other drives him to consider the role social institutions can play in addressing these vast inequalities. Against those who think that this problem can be addressed through "individual initiative alone and the mere free play of competition," he stresses that it will be necessary for individuals and intermediary bodies, with coordination by the state, to develop programs that will "encourage, stimulate, coordinate, supplement, and integrate" development for all persons.[49] While he is clear that development includes economic development, he is equally clear that development is not limited to economic development. True development addresses the *whole* person as well as the society. Understood in this way, development addresses social inequalities, discrimination, unjust working conditions, inadequate education, and poverty, while also encouraging the spiritual growth of the person.[50] He underscores that conventional methods of measuring economic development (i.e., GDP) do not take into account its distribution. True development, economic or otherwise, demands that *all* persons receive and contribute to the social and economic goods of their society and that, on a global scale, societies contribute to the well-being of the larger human family.

John Paul II: Affirming and Redefining Ownership in the Information Age

John Paul II's papacy (1978–2005) was the second longest in the history of the Roman Catholic Church. He witnessed momentous political, social, and economic change across the globe. During his papacy, the Soviet Union collapsed and their control loosened over a variety of Eastern European and other client states around the world. Significantly, John Paul's encouragement of the Polish solidarity movement was believed to be an important factor in the demise of the Soviet Union.[51] The importance and value he gives to work is no doubt influenced by his experience of state-controlled economic systems which limited individual initiative and human creativity, subordinating work completely to the goals and needs of the state. The Polish solidarity movement modeled two aspects of John Paul's social teaching, which he especially emphasizes in his social encyclicals: solidarity and subsidiarity. This same experience helps to explain, at least in part, his sharp criticism of aspects of liberation theology, particularly those that he saw as more Marxist than Christian.[52]

At the same time, John Paul was not an uncritical advocate of capitalism. While he gave conditional support to market-based economies, he was nevertheless highly critical of certain practices associated with capitalism. His approach to private property and ownership is both consistent with the earlier social teaching tradition and highly innovative.

Many of his revisions to the tradition are related to the dramatic shifts in the world's economies that increasingly privilege the creative use of intellectual assets.

John Paul was the author of three social encyclicals: *Laborum Exercens* (On Human Work), *Sollicitudo Rei Socialis* (On Social Concern), and *Centesimus Annus* (On the Hundredth Anniversary of *Rerum Novarum*). The first and third of these documents were written on the ninetieth and one hundredth anniversaries of *Rerum Novarum* respectively, while the second was written to commemorate the twentieth anniversary of *Populorum Progressio*. While John Paul addresses issues of ownership in all three of these documents, his most extensive treatment of the issue occurs in *Centesimus Annus*.

The priority given to the discussion of private property in *Centesimus Annus* reflects the emphasis that John Paul had given to the subject throughout his papacy. As Daniel Finn writes, in the pope's analysis of modern economic life "only the notion of the dignity of the human person is appealed to more frequently than the teaching on private property."[53] Following the papal social tradition, John Paul II affirms "the natural character of the right to private property."[54] Likewise, he notes that the Church has long held that this right is not absolute and he suggests that private property carries with it social obligations. As he puts it, private property has a "social mortgage."[55] As with previous popes, John Paul II believed that "the use of privately owned goods was subject to strict limits because the material world was created by God for the benefit of all human beings, not just a few."[56] This is what is meant by the phrase "universal destination of material goods." As John Paul puts it:

> The original source of all that is good is the very act of God, who created both the earth and man, and who gave the earth to man so that he might have dominion over it by his work and enjoy its fruits (Gen. 1:28). God gave the earth to the whole human race for the sustenance of all its members, without excluding or favoring anyone. This is the foundation of the universal destination of the earth's goods. The earth, by reason of its fruitfulness and its capacity to satisfy human needs, is God's first gift for the sustenance of human life.[57]

While the notion that the goods of the earth belong to all has been central to the tradition's teaching on private property, John Paul subtly shifts the language of this tradition so that he speaks not of a right *of* private property but rather a right *to* private property. The early papal social encyclicals were frequently criticized for appearing to be apologia for the property class. John Paul's formulation of property rights makes it clear that all persons have a "claim on property, a right to have sufficient amounts of it to maintain themselves and those for whom they have responsibility."[58]

By his own account John Paul's treatment of the tradition's understanding of private property is "reread" in light of economic and technological developments in the modern world. This "deeper analysis"[59] of the relationship between individual or private property and the universal destination of material wealth leads him to extend the concept of property to include not just material things but also personal capacities such as ideas, creativity, and skills. "In our time, in particular, there exists another form of ownership which is becoming no less important than land: the possession of know-how, technology and skill."[60] Original meanings of private property were linked almost exclusively to land, but only through the application of intelligence and work does the land become fruitful. As Leo did before him, John Paul asserts that this is how human beings make the earth their own: "This is the origin of individual property."[61] However, John Paul reformulates this understanding of property ownership in line with new developments in modern economies in which intelligence and creativity take on far greater importance.

The importance given to these human capacities in contemporary economies carries with it a particular danger, however. Those who are able to successfully exploit the use of creative intelligence will attribute the fruits of their work solely to their own personal agency. As David Hollenbach observes, "This would undercut the limits on the right to private property asserted by the earlier tradition."[62] An important part of the rationale for placing limits on the right to private property was that the goods that one possessed were not solely of one's own making. This, John Paul makes clear, is also true for personal capacities such as intelligence, skill, and ingenuity, the development of which is dependent upon the wider human community. So, for example, the medical doctor today benefits from a vast array of knowledge without which the practice of the profession would be impossible. Similarly, this same doctor depends upon a complex array of businesses that are essential in applying the knowledge that he or she possesses. Knowing that penicillin or another antibiotic can treat bacterial infection is of little use without the pharmaceutical company that produces it.

An analogous dependency and interconnectedness applies to the scientist working for the pharmaceutical company that develops and manufactures new drugs, or to any professional whose product is primarily intellectual. Even in cases where it appears that individuals are acting solely out of their own imagination to create an entirely new product or service, their endeavor is vitally linked to the society and community that has educated and supported them. Thus, for example, those who founded the technology company Google could not have done so without the vast body of publicly funded technological research or the entire infrastructure of the internet upon which their service depends.

John Paul extends this basic idea to all levels of economic activity. Thus, for example, persons working within a corporation depend upon those within the corporation for the exercise of their various capacities. His analysis reflects the Catholic social tradition's recognition of the inherent sociality and interdependence of human beings. "By means of his work man commits himself, not only for his own sake but also for others and with others. Each person collaborates in the work of others and for their good. Man works in order to provide for the needs of his family, his community, his nation, and ultimately all humanity."[63]

Despite the new importance given to intellectual property, many are denied or prevented from developing the means to generate or acquire it. John Paul recognizes that the vast majority of the human population is excluded from participating in this vital arena. As he so poignantly puts it:

> The fact is that many people, perhaps the majority today, do not have the means which would enable them to take their place in an effective and humanly dignified way within a productive system in which work is truly central. They have no possibility of acquiring the basic knowledge which would enable them to express their creativity and develop their potential. They have no way of entering the network of knowledge and intercommunication which would enable them to see their qualities appreciated and utilized. Thus, if not actually exploited, they are to a great extent marginalized; economic development takes place over their heads, so to speak, when

it does not actually reduce the already narrow scope of their old subsistence economies.[64]

The emergence of economies primarily dependent upon technological know-how and creative applications of human intelligence exacerbates the condition of those who were marginalized or exploited by earlier economic paradigms. As John Paul notes, "for the poor, to the lack of material goods has been added a lack of knowledge and training which prevents them from escaping their state of humiliating subjection."[65]

In linking "know-how, technology, and skill" to the universal destination of material goods, the pope, as David Hollenbach observes, is not only broadening the meaning of property so that it now includes intellectual property, but he is also signaling that the latter is "not the purely private possession of anyone." Rather, these capacities "are meant to be at the service of others. They should be used to open up ways for the vast numbers of people who are marginalized from the markets to become active participants in it."[66] As John Paul puts it, in "the light of today's 'new things,' we have reread the relationship between individual or private property and the universal destination of material wealth. Man fulfills himself by using his intelligence and freedom. In so doing he utilizes the things of this world as objects and instruments and makes them his own. The foundation of the right to private initiative and ownership is to be found in this activity."[67]

To the degree that assets contribute to the ability to develop skills and fund education and training, they remain an important element in fighting poverty. Assets can enable entrance into the network of creative entrepreneurship from which the poor are excluded. The real purpose of assets in the twenty-first century is precisely to enable and empower people to develop and deploy their human as well as financial capital. A just asset-building policy would ensure that the poor are enabled to develop the skills necessary to participate in the modern economy.

U.S. Catholic Bishops: Economic Justice

One final example of Catholic social teaching comes from a local ecclesial body—the National Conference of Catholic Bishops (NCCB). Some two decades ago, the NCCB published *Economic Justice For All*, a clarion call to Roman Catholics and the nation to address the economic challenges faced by so many in the United States and around the world.[68] Those challenges included the fact that 33 million people were living in poverty with "another 20–30 million" judged needy "by any reasonable standard."[69] The bishops also noted "many working people and middle-class Americans live dangerously close to poverty" and that, over a ten-year period, "nearly a quarter of the U.S. population was in poverty part of the time and received welfare benefits in at least one year."[70] To this account of material deprivation, the bishops added that the U.S. economy "is marked by very uneven distribution of wealth and income." With respect to wealth distribution, 2 percent of the nation's families controlled 28 percent of the total net wealth and 54 percent of the nation's net financial assets. The bishops noted that inequalities in income distribution, although not quite as severe as inequalities in wealth distribution, were nevertheless significant. the top 20 percent of income earners received nearly 43 percent of the nation's income, while the bottom 40 percent received only 15.7 percent.[71] The degree of inequality of wealth and income in the United States, the bishops suggested ominously, could become "a threat to the solidarity of the human community, for great disparities lead to deep social divisions and conflict."[72] These and other troubling aspects of economic conditions in the United States and around the world led the bishops to characterize the current state of affairs as "a social and moral scandal," one that they "could not ignore."[73]

In the course of addressing the underlying economic structures that were contributing to the vast disparities in the distribution of wealth and income, high levels of poverty, and unemployment, *Economic Justice for All* articulates a number of overarching goals toward which economic policy should aim. These include reducing levels of poverty and inequality by expanding opportunities for, and eliminating obstacles to, adequate paying work and raising the minimum wage for those who do work.

> The first line of attack against poverty must be to build and sustain a healthy economy that provides employment opportunities at just wages for all adults who are able to work. Poverty is intimately linked to the issue of employment. Millions are poor because they have lost their jobs or because their wages are too low. The persistent high levels of unemployment during the last decade are a major

reason why poverty has increased. . . . In recent years the minimum wage has not been adjusted to keep pace with inflation. Its real value has declined by 24 percent since 1981. We believe Congress should raise the minimum wage in order to restore some of the purchasing power it has lost due to inflation.[74]

For "so long as we tolerate a situation in which people can work full time and still be below the poverty line—a situation common among those earning the minimum wage—too many will continue to be counted among the 'working poor.' Concerted efforts must be made through job training, affirmative action, and other means to assist those now prevented from obtaining more lucrative jobs."[75] The bishops also recognize that if poverty is to be reduced, society must ensure access to adequate benefits and working conditions such as those employed in more lucrative positions routinely receive. "The dignity of workers also requires adequate health care, security for old age or disability, unemployment compensation, healthful working conditions, weekly rest, periodic holidays for recreation and leisure, and reasonable security against arbitrary dismissal" and "[e]mployers, governments, and private agencies need to improve both the availability and the quality of child care services."[76]

At the same time, the bishops went beyond this "income paradigm" approach when they called for expanding *ownership* to greater numbers of persons and families. Just as they recognized that public policy has a role to play in raising income levels of the poor (and in facilitating access to better paying jobs), they also recognized that public policy has a role to play in expanding ownership—"efforts that *enable the poor to participate in the ownership and control of economic resources* are especially important."[77] The development of "policies and programs that support family life and enhance economic participation through employment *and* widespread ownership of property" is needed.[78]

From the beginning, property and ownership have played a central role in the Catholic social tradition. The emphasis has been on expanding ownership to those without property as a means of reducing levels of poverty. The goods of the earth belong to all, and therefore all persons have a rightful claim to an adequate level of those goods. Likewise, those that labor have a rightful claim to a share of the goods that they produce. While these documents make it clear that an adequate or rightful share of the goods ought to be in the form of adequate remuneration, the latter is almost always defined in terms of both wages and ownership.

CONTRIBUTIONS OF CATHOLIC SOCIAL THOUGHT TO ASSET-BUILDING POLICY

Modern Catholic social teaching addresses itself to a number of areas of social concern including, as we have seen, economic justice. Across all areas of social concern Catholic social thought employs certain basic moral and theological principles in developing its moral analysis. It is the commitment to these principles that explains the Church's concern regarding economic issues. These same principles can help to provide a moral framework for asset-building policy.

As noted at the beginning of this chapter, the success of public policy initiatives related to issues of social justice often depends upon the persuasiveness of the moral argument that supports the policy. For this reason, it is not enough to simply assert that the tradition of Catholic social thought endorses the idea of asset-building for the poor. To be fully understood, the claims of Catholic social thought regarding ownership need to be situated in relation to the fundamental principles that animate the tradition. These basic principles can also provide a moral framework for asset-building policies and add a dimension to the discussion that is currently generally absent or muted.

Providing such a framework is important for a number of reasons. First, grounding these policies in substantive ethical principles helps to give a more secure foundation to the moral reasoning already implicit in asset building. This foundation is important, not only to provide resources for persuasive public argument in support of asset-building policies for the poor, but also to prevent these latter kinds of policies from being co-opted and used for purposes for which they were never intended. This is not an idle concern as the 2004 debate in the United States about the creation of an "ownership society" demonstrated. Using the language of asset building, influential persons advocated policies that favored the wealthy over the poor and thus turned the intent of the asset-building approach on its head. Catholic social thought could provide a helpful critique and corrective by directing policy in ways that are compassionate and sensitive to those most in need. It can help to set limits and boundaries regarding what is legitimate and illegitimate use of the language and ideas behind the asset-building approach.

Catholic social thought also provides a needed counterbalance and corrective to the emphasis, in this country at least, on "rugged individualism" and the myth of pulling oneself up by one's bootstraps. Its strong emphasis on the social nature of the person underscores the interdependent and interrelated nature of human affairs and the centrality of institutions in facilitating human endeavor. The importance it gives to the constitutive nature of human relationships promotes the virtue of solidarity with others and helps explain the value of coming to the assistance of those in need.

In addition, including Catholic social thought in asset-building discussions may bring into the conversation significant sectors of the population who are disengaged or focused on other social issues. If the Church were to enter into the growing policy debate about asset building, this could provide the opportunity for a "teachable moment." In the United States, significant numbers of Catholics (and non-Catholics) are unfamiliar with the economic teachings of the Church and would likely be startled by many of the claims it makes. It would be no small achievement to introduce or reintroduce these important teachings and thereby broaden the current debate.

Key principles, values, and commitments that support the Church's teaching on ownership include human dignity, the social nature of the person, the common good, human freedom, and the preferential option for the poor. These may well prove useful to those currently developing asset-building policies.

Human Dignity

The Church's commitment to the dignity of the person is the basis for all of its social teaching, including its teaching on economic matters. Informed by scripture and other sources, the Church views the person as a material, moral, intellectual, and spiritual being. These qualities are not separate and distinct from one another, but integrally related. While endowed with capacities for freedom and transcendence, human beings are embodied creatures with material needs that must be met if they are to flourish. Their material well-being cannot be ignored even by those whose central concern is spiritual. Nor can those human activities which focus on the production of material things ignore the spiritual dimension of the human person. Economies are to be evaluated according to how well they serve all aspects of the human person who is "the source, the center, and the purpose of all socioeconomic life."[79]

Catholic social thought calls for a re-visioning of the economic sphere to one informed more by biblical norms, religious principles, and philosophical reflection on the nature of personhood than by the mechanistic language of many economists. Against those who argue that economic decisions ought to be driven by purely "market" considerations (i.e., maximizing efficiency, productivity, profitability, and so on), Catholic social teaching insists that the criterion for evaluating an economic decision is "whether it protects or undermines the dignity of the human person."[80] That dignity is grounded in the biblical claim that human persons are created in the image of God, the *imago dei*. As the U.S. Catholic bishops note, "Every human person is created as an image of God, and the denial of dignity to a person is a blot on this image."[81] Catholic social teaching is clear that "in the socioeconomic realm . . . the dignity . . . of the human person must be honored and advanced along with the welfare of society as a whole."[82]

Human dignity demands that people be treated with equal regard and respect. As those terms are applied to the social and political order today, they are usually understood to encompass political liberties alone. Within the Catholic social tradition, however, equal regard and respect demand more. As William O'Neill explains, "respect for persons *as* moral agents implies, *a fortiori*, respect for the conditions of their exercising agency (i.e., the provision of basic liberties and welfare)"; persons are "entitled, not merely to 'negative' liberties, but to basic welfare-rights."[83] That is, the rights recognized by Catholic social thought include not only social and political rights but also economic rights. Persons not only have rights to assemble, to speak freely in public, and to vote, they also have the right to participate in the economic sphere and to a share of the goods of the economy. All of these things are understood as necessary for the protection and promotion of human dignity. As the Second Vatican Council observed, "There is a growing awareness of the sublime dignity of human persons, who stand above all things and whose rights and duties are universal and inviolable. They ought, therefore, to have ready access to all that is necessary for living a genuinely human life: for example, food, clothing, housing, . . . the right to education, and work. . . ."[84] Moreover, social and political institutions have a positive obligation to secure these rights and the goods associated with them for all persons. For example, the right to private property cannot simply be asserted abstractly, it must be realized in practice.[85] In sum, since human dignity and the exercise of freedom are mutually implicating, one cannot respect the former without enabling the exercise of the latter.

The Social Nature of the Person

While human dignity is foundational, based on the *imago dei,* and prior to any personal achievement or accomplishment, it is nevertheless actualized and secured in association with other human beings. The strong emphasis within this tradition on the social nature of the person can be traced to both biblical and philosophical influences. From scripture, the tradition points to the fact that humans are fundamentally social, created in relationship first and foremost to God and not meant to be alone (Gen. 1–2). This same biblical tradition recounts the story of the Exodus in which Hebrew slaves were freed from political and economic oppression and subsequently joined together into a community:

> God did not create man for life in isolation, but for the formation of social unity. So also "it has pleased God to make men holy and save them not merely as individuals, without any mutual bonds, but by making them into a single people, a people which acknowledges him in truth and serves him in holiness." So from the beginning of salvation history he has chosen men not just as individuals but as members of a certain community. Revealing his mind to them, God called these chosen ones "His people" (Exod. 3:7–12), and, furthermore, made a covenant with them on Sinai.[86]

Central to the Christian understanding of community is the Exodus event and the establishment of a covenant at Sinai. Prior to the Exodus, Israel lacked a community—they were simply a dispersed group of slaves. As such they were denied their dignity as persons. When God called Israel out of Egypt, God established a covenant with them and gave them the Law. The Law, according to the U.S. bishops, is what made community possible.

Far from being an arbitrary restriction on the life of the people, these codes [contained in the Decalogue (Ex. 20:1–17) and the Book of the Covenant (Ex. 20:22–23:33)] made life in community possible. The specific laws of the covenant protect human life and property, demand respect for parents and the spouses and children of one's neighbor, and manifest a special concern for the vulnerable members of the community: widows, orphans, the poor, and strangers in the land.[87]

That God goes to such extraordinary lengths to provide a community for all of Israel, not just a few of the more powerful, indicates that God intends community as an essential aspect of human life. All persons, regardless of their particular status in the society, need community. To the extent that a society and its social structures (e.g., the economy) function in such a way as to push people to the edges of society, it keeps those persons who are marginalized from fully participating in community, and, hence, from fully experiencing their humanity. Therefore,

[b]asic justice demands the establishment of minimum levels of participation in the life of the human community for all persons. The ultimate injustice is for a person or group to be treated actively or abandoned passively as if they were nonmembers of the human race. To treat people this way is effectively to say they simply do not count as human beings.[88]

The U.S. bishops, in a brief but important passage, also make reference to the *imago dei* to support the essential communal nature of human persons. If persons are created in the image of God and God is understood as a "trinitarian union of persons" this reveals that "being a person means being united to other persons in mutual love."[89]

The Catholic social tradition has typically grounded its moral arguments not only in scripture but also in the tradition of natural law. This tradition was heavily influenced by Thomas Aquinas and, through him, the philosophy of Aristotle. Like the biblical tradition, Aristotle and Aquinas interpret the person as essentially social and therefore place a very high value on community. Both Aristotle and Aquinas argued that human beings are essentially social and political, interdependent, and are not fully realized apart from participation in community. As Aristotle asserted, "He who is unable to live in society, or who has no need because he is sufficient for himself, must be either a beast or a god."[90] In his commentary on Aristotle's *Politics*, Thomas Aquinas endorses Aristotle's claim:

> The fact that man is by nature a social animal—being compelled to live in society because of the many needs he cannot satisfy out of his own resources—has as a consequence the fact that man is destined by nature to form part of a community which makes a full and complete life possible for him. The help of such a communal life is necessary to him for two reasons. In the first place it is necessary to provide him with those things without which life itself would be impossible. For this purpose there is the domestic community of which man forms a part. We all get life and food and education from our parents, and it is thus that the various individuals of a family assist one another with what is necessary to existence. But life in a community further enables man to achieve a plenitude of life; not merely to exist, but to live fully, with all that is necessary to well-being. In this sense the political community, of which man forms a part, assists him not merely to obtain material comforts, such as are produced by the many diverse industries of a state, but also spiritual well-being, as when youthful intemperance, which paternal admonishment is unable to control, is restrained by public authority.[91]

The Catholic social tradition generally believes that there is a harmony between the natural law and what scripture teaches. Thus, for example, the U.S. bishops argue that their biblically derived vision of the human person as essentially communal is in agreement with secular philosophical thought. "What the Bible and Christian tradition teach, human wisdom confirms. Centuries before Christ, the Greeks and Romans spoke of the human person as a 'social animal' made for friendship, community, and public life. These insights show that human beings achieve self-realization not in isolation, but in interaction with others."[92]

In sum, within Catholic social thought, human beings have particular rights and freedoms, including economic rights, and are intended to exercise those rights and freedoms in community with other people. Indeed, all persons have the *right* to community. The economy which seeks to make such a life possible for all persons is a just economy.

Given the immense importance of society and social institutions to the well-being of persons, political and economic institutions play a key role in peoples' lives. These institutions are integral to the flourishing of persons. As noted by the Second Vatican Council,

> Man's social nature makes it evident that the progress of the human person and the advance of society itself hinge on each other. For the beginning, the subject, and the goal of all social institutions is and must be the human person, which for its part and by its very nature stands completely in need of social life. This social life is not something added on to man. Hence, through his dealings with others, through reciprocal duties, and through fraternal dialogue he develops all his gifts and is able to rise to his destiny.[93]

The Common Good

The recognition of the social nature of the person finds expression in another important theme in Catholic social thought, that of the common good. In contrast to many forms of modern political liberalism that see an inherent tension or even an incompatibility between the demands of the community and individual freedom, the Catholic tradition views the good of the individual and the good of the community as integrally related. John XXIII defines the common good as "the sum total of those conditions of social living, whereby persons are enabled more fully and readily to achieve their own perfection."[94] The "perfection" that human beings realize is not and cannot be achieved in isolation; it is a good that is dependent upon relationship with others and, as David Hollenbach points out, "this shared life of communication and interaction with others, in all its aspects, is good in itself."[95] In other words, the common good cannot be broken down into individual goods but is a shared good that emerges from the participation of all for the good of all. To the degree that ownership is correlated with greater participation at all levels of society, expanding the number of owners not only contributes to the individual good of these new owners but also to the good of all members of society.

Unless participants in the body politic and the social institutions they create really do prioritize the good of all, they can become a barrier to human flourishing. When socioeconomic and political institutions provide unfair advantages to some, while discriminating against others, these institutions foster and perpetuate unjust inequalities in ways that deny the dignity of all persons. Commenting on "the situation of inhuman poverty in which millions of Latin Americans live as the most devastating and humiliating kind of scourge," the bishops of Latin America highlight the structural nature of their deprivation. This deprivation, which takes the form of high rates "of infant mortality, a lack of adequate housing, health problems, starvation wages, unemployment and underemployment, malnutrition, job uncertainty, compulsory mass migrations, etc." is not accidental or simply a "passing phase." It is instead "the product of economic, social, and political situations and structures" which "create a situation on the international level where the rich get richer at the expense of the poor, who get ever poorer."[96]

Human Freedom

Catholic social thought most frequently discusses the question of ownership in the context of enabling human freedom. In the Catholic tradition human freedom is not primarily associated with freedom *from* interference by the state and others, nor is it simply the freedom to do as one pleases. Rather, the notion of human freedom has a much more social meaning and therefore includes the freedom to contribute to and participate in society as well as the freedom to enjoy the benefits of that society. A distinctive quality of human freedom involves the capacity to plan and make decisions about the future direction of our lives. The Catholic social tradition acknowledges that an important aspect of ownership is that it enables persons to plan and make decisions about their future. Those who are living at a subsistence level will find it far more difficult to engage in this kind of future-oriented activity and in this way will find their freedom curtailed. Asset ownership thus can be seen to be integral to the promotion of human freedom.

Pius XII asserts that the dignity of the human person "normally demands the right to the use of the goods of the earth, to which corresponds the fundamental obligation of granting an opportunity to possess property to all if possible."[97] John XXIII contends that the right to private ownership of property is "a means of asserting one's personality and exercising responsibility in every field" as well as "an element of solidity and security for family life and of greater peace and prosperity in the State."[98] Similarly, *Gaudium et Spes* argues that "[p]rivate property or some ownership of external goods confers on everyone a sphere wholly necessary for the autonomy of the person and the family, and it should be regarded as an extension of human freedom." In addition, ownership "adds incentives for carrying on one's function and charge" and therefore "it constitutes one of the conditions for civil liberties."[99] For their part, the U.S. Catholic bishops repeatedly stress the importance of expanding ownership to as many people as possible. Since human freedom depends not only on a certain level of material well-being but also on the enabling of participation in human society, including participation in the economy, priority should be given "to policies and programs that support family life and enhance economic participation through employment and widespread ownership of property."[100] In a different context, the bishops endorse an earlier statement made by their fellow bishops in 1919: "the full possibilities of increased production will not be realized so long as the majority of workers remain mere wage earners. The majority must somehow become owners, at least in part, of the instruments of production."[101] The bishops add that "[w]e believe that this judgment remains generally valid today."[102]

But the U.S. bishops show a more sophisticated awareness than their earlier colleagues of the institutional relationships that enhance the economic well-being of some while denying it to others. However, despite this awareness of the institutional barriers to ownership, the bishops, along with much of Catholic social teaching, still assume a neoclassical model of saving and therefore an overly individualistic understanding of how persons save and accumulate assets. This leads them to overlook the powerful social determinants of saving and how these might be used to enable the poor to save. It also contributes to a truncated notion of the meaning of economic participation, which the bishops associate primarily with employment. To be a participant in today's economy, one must have more than a job. One must have access to all of those financial institutions and mechanisms that facilitate ownership. Those who do not have access to, and the freedom to participate in, these dimensions of economic life cannot be said to be "included" in society, even if they have gainful employment.

Preferential Option for the Poor

The preferential option for the poor has become increasingly important in modern Catholic social thought. The first explicit development of this theme occurred in the *Final Document* of the Third General Conference of Latin American Bishops in 1979. This document included a chapter titled "The Preferential Option for the Poor."[103] The basic concept can be traced back to the Bible. Both the Hebrew and Christian scriptures state again and again that God has a special concern for the poor, downtrodden, marginalized, and oppressed. This concern is not portrayed as peripheral to the God of Jews and Christians. Rather, God's concern for the poor is central to the biblical narrative. Central to the defining narrative of the Jewish faith—the Exodus—is the idea that God is moved by the cries of his people, a people who are portrayed as enslaved, impoverished, and socially and politically disempowered. The story of the Exodus is a story of liberation, a liberation that includes freedom from material deprivation. Concern for the poor is also central to the Christian story. In the Gospels, Jesus is portrayed repeatedly as one who has a special concern for the poor and the marginalized of his society. His identification with the poor is perhaps best exemplified in the well-known biblical text "whatever you do to the least of these you do to me" (Matthew 25:40–41).

The distinctive contribution of the concept of the preferential option for the poor is to call attention to the importance of giving primacy to the needs of the poor. This primacy occurs at several levels. Affectively, it involves a love of the poor that manifests, as John Paul II put it, through an "option, or a *special form* of primacy in the exercise of Christian charity."[104] Morally, it involves a reorientation of value from one that places a higher value on things than persons. Practically, it involves a shift in policy that places the needs of the poor at the center of public concern. As John Paul II observed,

> given the worldwide dimension which the social question has assumed, this love of preference for the poor, and the decisions which it inspires in us, cannot but embrace the immense multitudes of the hungry, the needy, the homeless, those without medical care and, above all, those without hope of a better future. It is impossible not to take account of the existence of these realities. To ignore them

would mean becoming like the "rich man" who pretended not to know the beggar Lazarus lying at his gate (cf. Luke 16:19–31).[105]

One of the clearest and most eloquent expressions of the implications of the preferential option is found in the U.S. Catholic bishops' letter on the economy: economic decisions "must be judged in light of what they do *for* the poor, what they do *to* the poor, and what they enable the poor to do *for themselves*. The fundamental moral criterion for all economic decisions, policies, and institutions is this: They must be at the service of *all people, especially the poor*."[106]

Because the concepts of human freedom and dignity, the social nature of the person, participation, and ownership are all interrelated in the Catholic social tradition, we should not be surprised to find them woven together in discussions on poverty. Properly understood, the defense of ownership is not an effort to suggest that ownership and the accumulation of assets is an end in itself. In the Catholic social tradition wealth is a means of enabling genuine human activity, including broader participation in the economic, civic, social, and political life of the community. For these reasons the bishops teach that "[e]fforts that enable the poor to participate in the ownership and control of economic resources are especially important."[107]

Despite the centrality of the concept of the preferential option in biblical texts and in the Church's social teaching, some Catholics and other Christians continue to express theological and ethical reservations about the preferential option for the poor. In brief, as Stephen Pope points out, the theological concern has to do with whether one can reconcile God's universal love with the notion that God shows a preference for some and not others. The ethical worry is related to the notion that impartiality and justice are inextricably linked. To be impartial is to be fair, unbiased, and resistant to favoritism. Partiality is associated with discrimination, a notion that has become closely identified with injustice. By contrast, the partiality denoted by the preferential option for the poor entails a principle of distributive justice, a principle that

> rests upon the belief that moral concern should be proportioned to need, where 'need' can be interpreted to include poverty, but also vulnerability, powerlessness, marginality, etc. Other things being equal, Christians should assign priority to addressing the needs of

the poor and otherwise powerless rather than to the needs of others because the former are by definition less capable of providing for themselves than are the latter. . . . This of course by no means suggests that the poor as people possess more worth than other people or that behavior that is morally wrong for others is morally acceptable when engaged in by the poor. . . .[108]

More generally, Pope argues that "partiality is justifiable when it contributes to inclusiveness." That is, when "the preferential option appeals to an *expansion* rather than *contraction* of love and wisdom"it is consistent with ethical and theological principles of the Catholic social tradition.[109]

CONTRIBUTIONS OF ASSET-BUILDING RESEARCH TO CATHOLIC SOCIAL THOUGHT

What does the asset-development approach to poverty contribute to Catholic social thought? In general, asset-building research offers a substantive and constructive critique of Catholic social thought while illuminating helpful pathways to achieve some of its essential aims.

First, asset-building literature provides a clear analytical distinction between the function of income and the function of assets or wealth. It marshals considerable empirical evidence to support these functional distinctions and makes clear the importance of asset development to human well-being. This functional distinction between income and wealth highlights the inherent value of wealth for all persons and helps to address a deep ambivalence to wealth present in Catholic social thought and in Christianity in general.

This ambivalence has been present in Christianity from its inception. We can see it in well-known scriptural passages which suggest on the one hand that wealth is a barrier to salvation, that material things are a source of temptation to sin, and on the other that the poor are God's chosen ones, favored in God's sight. As Carter Lindberg observes, in early Christianity it is not so much poverty that is the problem but wealth: "As middle- and upper-class people entered the early Christian community, the obvious bias of the gospel toward the poor raised the question, so succinctly expressed by the famous sermon of Clement of Alexandria:

'How is the rich man to be saved?'"[110] For many, the answer to this question is "by giving alms to the poor" thus establishing a "symbiotic relationship between rich and poor," in which the latter become the means to the salvation of the former. According to Lindberg,

> The medieval preachers and theologians did not hesitate to refer to this relationship of the rich to the poor as a commercial transaction—the poor carry the riches of the wealthy on their backs to heaven. *The* theologian of the medieval church, Augustine, had stated: "If our possessions are to be carried away, let us transfer them to a place where we shall not lose them. The poor to whom we give alms! With regard to us, what else are they but porters through whom we transfer our goods from earth to heaven? Give away your treasure. Give it to the porter. He will bear it to heaven what you give him on earth."[111]

Thus there is a deep-seated ambivalence in Christianity not only regarding wealth, but also the elimination of poverty and the poor. If the poor are regarded as a vehicle of salvation for the wealthy, then the elimination of poverty will be viewed on some level as a threat. What the asset-building literature suggests is that some degree of wealth is necessary for the protection and promotion of human dignity. This observation challenges the Christian tradition's ambivalence toward wealth creation, especially for the poor.

The symbiotic relationship between the rich and the poor has contributed to an overemphasis on charity and almsgiving as a means to address poverty. Such charity may help to ameliorate some of the pernicious effects of poverty, but it can never be an adequate solution, only a stopgap measure to address immediate needs. The preferential option for the poor provides a crucial moral warrant for systematically addressing poverty, but not if it is understood primarily in terms of charity. It must be adjusted and nuanced to allow for sustainable opportunities for economic participation for all members of a given society.

Second, the distinction between income and assets also helps to identify in a clear and precise way important mechanisms of exclusion in contemporary economic arrangements. This analysis helps bolster Catholic social thought's already cogent critique of institutional arrangements that materially enrich the lives of the few who least need it while impeding the development of the many who most need it. The specificity of the analysis in the asset-building field with respect to particular mechanisms of wealth creation underscores the need for Catholic social thought to go deeper in its own assessment of the problem of poverty and to approach solutions with more concrete prescriptions. It is not that Catholic social thought fails to recognize the importance of expanding ownership to as many persons as possible, but that not enough attention is given to particular policy mechanisms that would enable such widespread ownership to become a reality. Because of this, proclamations that all should become owners can seem to be an empty ideal. The tendency of Catholic social thought to produce general recommendations about expanding ownership does not help to illuminate specific public pathways that could actually expand ownership to the poor. Just as important, it obscures mechanisms of ownership for those who are nonpoor. Going forward, the Church can draw on asset-building research, in a way that both Catholics and non-Catholics can endorse, to bolster and concretize its case that ownership should be much more widespread.

Put another way, Catholic social thought has long recognized that adequate material resources are a necessary, although not sufficient, aspect of human flourishing. For this reason, it has a long tradition of supporting both a "living" or "family" wage and private ownership. There is, however, a tendency to blur the distinction between income and income transfers and assets and ownership by assuming that there is a necessary relationship between the two—that is, that sufficient income will inexorably lead to ownership. It has not articulated with a degree of specificity the important role that institutions and social policies play in facilitating individual ownership. Catholic social thought recognizes that policy has an important influence on expanding ownership, but shows little awareness of the degree to which the nonpoor are being subsidized in their efforts to accumulate assets and the poor are not. Given both the consistent emphasis that Catholic social thought places on the role that social institutions play in facilitating or impeding human well-being and the extent of its discussions regarding the benefits of ownership, those working within the Catholic social tradition should take a closer look at its programmatic recommendations regarding ownership and the poor. Here again, research on asset development is extremely helpful.

Third, by studying mechanisms of exclusion and marginalization, asset-building research identifies another dimension of what it means to participate in modern economies. As previously noted, a central idea in Catholic social thought is the important connection between the protection and promotion of human dignity and the idea of participation in society. Persons should be enabled and allowed to participate in society, and this includes participation in the economic life of society. Given the importance of savings and investments to one's economic well-being in general, the growing importance of savings vehicles in a postindustrial economy, and the widening wealth gap between the rich and the poor, a strong case can be made that full participation in the economy requires more than simply paid employment; it requires access to financial institutions and savings plans as well.

As Catholic social thought developed during the twentieth century, greater emphasis was placed on the value of work and less emphasis on the value of ownership. Certainly part of the reason for this change in emphasis can be traced to the shift from an agrarian economy to an industrial and now postindustrial economy. When land was the primary generator of income, land ownership was understood to be crucial to economic well-being. As land became less central to income generation, ownership tended to receive less attention. Yet asset ownership remains integral to economic well-being and the recognition of the dignity of work does not change this reality. Given the evident positive psychosocial aspects of asset ownership in all of its forms (e.g., land, real estate, cash reserves, securities and other financial instruments, partnerships, pensions, and so on) and the role that asset ownership plays in fully facilitating participation in modern economies, Catholic social thought needs once again to underscore the value of ownership and the importance of expanding it to all.

Given the suspicion that some hold toward modern market economies, the recommendation that the poor be given greater access to financial instruments and institutions may be met with ambivalence or even active opposition. Since market economies are held by some to be the cause of widespread poverty, encouraging the poor to participate would likely be seen to exacerbate the problem. Such concerns are not unreasonable, as the current mortgage crisis attests. Here, under the guise of extending ownership to a wider segment of the population, poorer people were exploited by subprime mortgage lenders without adequate social policies or regulations in place that would help to support and sustain ownership and limit risk to the most vulnerable. These problems are real and they have a long history. This was not the first mortgage crisis and it will not be the last. Other examples of abuses within market economies abound. Nevertheless, market economies provide important economic benefits and the goal ought to be to expand these benefits to as many persons as possible. Policies that help the poor to save and accumulate assets offer a promising mechanism through which the ideals of Catholic social thought can be effectively realized.

The Catholic social tradition contains significant resources for moral reflection on the nature of human economic activity, but whether and how its moral insights ought to be brought to bear on public policy in a pluralistic democracy depends to a considerable degree on the persuasiveness of the claims it makes.

To some degree, the persuasiveness of these insights depends upon the authority that any particular person grants to the Catholic Church, its official spokespersons, and their supporting texts and resources. The bishops' analysis of the U.S. economy will initially be granted more authority by Catholics than non-Catholics, although this is by no means universally true.[112] Similarly, an argument grounded in a particular biblical text may be more persuasive to those who accept that the Bible is in some way the revealed Word of God. But, again, this is not necessarily the case. It is quite plausible that someone who rejects the claim that scripture is the product of divine revelation may nevertheless find that the Bible contains important insights into the human condition. And even those who accept the divine authority of scripture differ in the relative value that they grant to particular texts within the Bible. In the latter case, the relative valuing of texts depends upon complex criteria which may or may not form a coherent interpretive matrix.[113]

The Catholic moral tradition has long maintained that reason and revelation do not contradict one another, and for a considerable period during its history much of its public moral argument relied almost exclusively on "reason" to support its moral claims. More recently, some moral theologians and Christian ethicists have called for a more explicitly Christian form of public argument since Christian symbols, stories, and texts can have moral resonance whether or not one subscribes to the Christian faith.[114] But another reason for increased calls for a more explicitly theological public discourse is that the once widely accepted claim that public debate ought to be dominated by "neutral" forms of rational argument (e.g., argument that did not depend upon "thickly" held conceptions of the good) has come to be seen as profoundly implausible. There is nothing neutral about procedures that require some to "bracket" or set aside constitutive beliefs and values while others are given free reign to appeal to alternative but far from neutral beliefs and values. For example, there is nothing neutral about marginalizing the claims of some who hold that the preferential option for the poor ought to be a guiding principle simply because it originates from within a religious tradition, while those who believe that all economic decisions should be left to "the invisible hand" of the market are granted unfettered access to the public sphere. The mere fact that an idea originates from within the social sciences does not mean it is any more neutral (or less value-laden) than ideas originating from religious traditions. Nevertheless theological ethics must be attuned to developments in the human sciences and other disciplines of human learning and remain open to the insights that these disciplines bring to moral endeavors.

CHAPTER THREE

Assets and Human Capabilities

If our world is to be a decent world in the future, we must acknowledge right now that we are citizens of one interdependent world, held together by mutual fellowship as well as the pursuit of mutual advantage, by compassion as well as by self-interest, by a love of human dignity in all people, even when there is nothing we have to gain from cooperating with them. Or rather, even when what we have to gain is the biggest thing of all: participation in a just and morally decent world.

—Martha Nussbaum, *Frontiers of Justice*

The Church's social teachings recognize that the dignity of the human person demands that all human beings have at least some minimum level of material well-being and that this minimum must include not only income, but savings and ownership. Some level of income *and* asset holdings enable persons to secure those goods that contribute to human development, both those necessary to sustain daily existence and those that develop the capabilities needed to live a fuller human life. In Catholic social teaching, individual well-being depends upon the capacity to give to and to receive from the social and political community in which one lives.

A complementary conception of social justice known as the "capabilities approach" is elaborated by Martha Nussbaum, one of the most influential contemporary American philosophers.[1] The capabilities approach holds that human beings share basic needs and capabilities which must be met and developed for human flourishing. According to Nussbaum, the role of human society is to develop and to enable the exercise of the capabilities of its members and so she places social justice at the center of her discussion. In so doing, she aims "to provide the philosophical underpinning for an account of core human entitlements that should be respected and implemented by the governments of all nations, as a bare minimum of what respect for human dignity requires."[2] She further explains that "[t]he capabilities are not understood as instrumental to a life with human dignity: they are understood, instead, as ways of realizing a life with human dignity, in the different areas of life with which human beings typically engage."[3] The basic question that needs to be asked of political, social, and economic institutions is what are they enabling people "to do and to be?"[4]

There are good reasons for considering the perspective of the capabilities approach on asset building for the poor alongside the social teachings of Roman Catholicism. First, the capabilities approach provides an additional and complementary rationale for many of the claims made in the Church's social teachings and in a way that is not tied to any particular theological tradition. This will help demonstrate that the asset-building approach can be defended morally both from *within* a particular religion's social teachings *and* from the perspective of a non-religious, philosophical approach to human well-being. A reasonable case for an asset-building approach to poverty alleviation can therefore be made without necessarily appealing to distinctive religious teachings of a particular tradition. This dual justification for asset building is especially important in societies characterized by what the philosopher John Rawls has called the "fact of reasonable pluralism," a social condition in which there are competing, reasonable, but incommensurable conceptions of the good human life.[5] Within this pluralism the Church offers a conception of the good life that some will find compatible with their own. The capabilities approach can contribute an alternative but complementary conception of social justice.

A second reason for focusing on the capabilities approach in the context of the Church's social teaching and asset building for the poor is that it can provide greater practical specificity to the Church's sometimes abstract assertions about the duties and responsibilities of human society to its members. The capabilities approach may, in other words, help to flesh out the implications for a given society of the Church's teachings regarding the things that any society ought to protect and promote. For example, the protection and promotion of human dignity is a central societal obligation and a society that fails to do this cannot be said to be a just one according to the social teachings of the Church. The capabilities approach can provide a reasonably comprehensive and specific set of criteria by which one can judge whether or not human dignity is being promoted or protected.

Third, like the Church's social teaching, the capabilities approach can remind persons why asset building for the poor is a necessary condition of social justice. To the degree that asset building facilitates the development of human capabilities there are good reasons to enable as many as possible to save and accumulate wealth. However, asset building is not an end in itself. The point of asset building is not to support ever increasing consumption but to help persons develop their human capabilities. Nussbaum is quite clear—as is the Catholic social justice tradition—that excessive material wealth can be an impediment to achieving the good human life. Beyond a certain level, society has no obligation to continue encouraging asset building and may well be justified in limiting the accumulation of assets in an effort to widen the sphere of persons who are enabled to accumulate assets and/or to encourage the development of vital capabilities.

A final reason for considering Nussbaum's capabilities approach is that many of those doing research and/or working on policy matters related to asset building for the poor view their work as consistent with the capabilities approach. Michael Sherraden argues, for example, that one thing distinguishing asset-building approaches to poverty alleviation from income-based approaches is the focus on

> *building capacities* for social and economic development more than on maintaining a certain level of consumption. Capacity building aims to increase individual and household resources, connections, knowledge, and abilities to function more effectively, to solve problems, and to increase well-being along multiple dimensions. The emphasis is on long-term development more than on maintenance of a current standard of living. The aim is to find interventions that provide a foundation for individuals' future growth and that eventually yield multiple positive outcomes.[6]

GLOBALIZATION AND THE NEED FOR A CROSS-CULTURAL ETHIC

One of the most significant changes of the last hundred years has been the increasing interconnectedness and interdependence of human beings around the globe. Because of these changes, people today are much more likely to be aware of cultural difference and variation within the world. They are also much more likely to be brought into contact with those whose religious, cultural, and historical background are significantly different from their own. These important and dramatic changes give an added urgency to the need for a normative, cross-cultural ethic even while the resources and credible arguments for such an ethic are being called into question. The inability to articulate and to put into practice such an ethic may increase the risk of misunderstanding and animosity between those who hold different worldviews and conceptions of the good. As "citizens of the world," the human community must be in a position to see what is common in each "other" and able to distinguish between that which is merely different and that which is harmful to the dignity and rights of persons.

Without such an ethic there are at least two risks: first, the risk of tolerating injustice because of a lack of a basis for critiquing it. This problem is occurring with greater and greater frequency, particularly among postmodern "liberal" thinkers, who interpret any critique of another cultural or religious practice as an unjust imposition of another culture's values.[7] Second, there is the risk of condemning behavior and practices that are not unjust but simply culturally variant expressions of moral behavior. These dangers are not new, but the increasing interdependence and interconnection of those who are "different" from each other increases opportunities for misunderstanding and mistaken judgments. Whether the mistaken judgment is facile toleration of injustices or an insensitive and inappropriate condemnation of differences, a contributing factor may be the lack of cross-cultural norms to determine whether or not a culture is impeding or enabling human flourishing. Postmodern thought— its attention drawn toward what is distinctive, different, and other— underscores dissimilarities but does not illuminate what is shared. What is needed is a conception of social justice that can accommodate and honor cultural differences, yet still argue for norms that cut across all cultures. Nussbaum's capabilities approach offers this possibility.

While the term 'postmodernism' covers a wide array of attitudes and dispositions toward modernity, most postmodern theories share a great skepticism toward "grand narratives," a deep suspicion of universal moral norms, and a tendency to emphasize difference and particularity over commonness and unity.[8] The underlying motivations for this stance are varied but two seem especially important. The first motivation is moral. A not unwarranted belief among postmodern thinkers is that "universal" principles and grand narratives have been used as vehicles for the powerful to oppress the powerless. This concern is rooted in, among other things, the historical realities of colonialism, slavery, the oppression of women, and prejudice of all kinds that were often justified through appeals to universal moral norms. As Jack Bonsor writes, "History is strewn with victims of the 'natural order.' Women, people of color, and homosexuals have been exploited, abused, and treated as chattel because this seemed nature's way."[9] The message of postmodernism is that such abuses can be avoided only by abandoning the quest for a universal conception of the human.

Nussbaum does not try to downplay this problem. Instead, she argues that a clear articulation of shared human capabilities minimizes the potential for abuse rather than aggravating it. She observes that discrimination has often been legitimated by those who argue that particular human beings or certain groups are, in fact, not human beings at all. She believes that the use of "a concrete and determinate list of elements" to define what all human beings have in common will help to make it difficult for such discrimination to occur.[10] A specific list of things recognized as the essential characteristics of human being increases the burden on those who would suggest that a certain group of beings that clearly meet these criteria are not human.

A second motivation for the postmodern critique of universalism is a philosophical one that has to do with the epistemological problems with making cross-cultural normative judgments about the good life. All knowledge, it is argued, is perspectival and so it is simply impossible to put forward some conception of the world or of persons as they actually are. There is no so-called reality "apart from the interpretive workings of the cognitive faculties of living beings", and these "interpretive workings" always belie the particular bias of individual historical, cultural, and social perspectives.[11] This critique is supported by the claim made by Richard Rorty and many others that human beings are "historical all the way through." This assertion has undermined what many have believed to be the necessary ground for any universal discourse: that in order to advance any kind of universal claim the human person must be understood as an

"ahistorical natural center . . . surrounded by an adventitious and ines-
sential periphery."[12] The growing acceptance of the historical nature of
the person and the consequent realization that all knowledge must be
perspectival has led to the conclusion that it is no longer tenable to advance the position that there is such a thing as a universal moral discourse. To suggest otherwise is, at best, a naïve mistake and, at worst, an
imperialistic imposition of one's own beliefs onto others.

Nussbaum responds to this concern by taking aim at the assump-
tion that a defense of universal moral norms must necessarily rely upon
an appeal to a transcendent, metaphysical ground. While Nussbaum
agrees that such appeals are no longer credible, she does not believe that
it is necessary to derive universal morals "independently of any experience of human life and history." The reason for this is that "universal
ideas of the human do arise within history and from human experience,
and they can ground themselves in experience."[13]

Her conception of the good life aims to give an account of persons
and the distinctive qualities they possess as they are known and encoun-
tered in history. In arguing for this "internal" account of the good, she
follows in the tradition of Aristotle who insisted that any account of the
good life should be one appropriate to human beings. As she points out,
Aristotle argues in the *Politics*, for example, that only human beings
have the sorts of ethical terms and concepts that we do "because the
beasts are unable to form the concepts, and gods lack the experiences of
limit and finitude that give a concept such as justice its point."[14]

In identifying essential characteristics of human beings Nussbaum
is looking for a universal conception of the human that is

> not metaphysical in the realist sense, nor extrahistorical, nor pecu-
> liar to a single metaphysical or religious tradition. It aims to be as
> universal as possible; indeed its guiding intuition directs it to cross
> religious and cultural gulfs. For it begins with two facts: first, that
> we recognize others as human across many divisions of time and
> place. . . . Second, we do have a broadly shared, general consensus
> about the features whose absence means the end of a human form
> of life.[15]

It follows, Nussbaum argues, that we remain capable of making normative judgments about the good human life, still able to see, as Aristotle

saw, that certain ways of living and understanding the world are better than others, and still able as well to judge that certain ways of living and understanding the world are "stupid, pernicious, and false."[16]

Nussbaum gives a persuasive and eloquent defense of the suitability of the Aristotelian approach to moral reflection in the postmodern age. She articulates an essentialist approach to ethical and political theory while remaining firmly planted in human experience. Her argument is universal without depending upon a priori arguments, existential without being relativistic. While respectful of cultural differences and the historical formation of the self, she stands firm against sectarianism. She remains convinced that human beings have more in common than what the postmodern critique would suggest and she points us in the direction of a social and political ethic that can deal with an increasingly interconnected and interdependent world.

A Thick, Vague Theory of the Good

Nussbaum's capabilities approach specifies a number of capacities and limits that she believes distinguish human beings from other life forms. Taken together, these capacities and limits delineate what she calls a "thick, vague" conception of the human good. In choosing to describe her conception of the good as "thick," she is consciously rejecting John Rawls's argument that in today's pluralistic world, where there are rival and incommensurable conceptions of the good and where it is no longer possible to appeal to transcendent, metaphysical grounds to resolve such conflicts, society must adopt a "thin" conception of the good. Rawls's minimalist approach to the good avoids taking a position on the purpose or end of human life precisely because the meaning and purpose of human life is so contested in the contemporary age. By contrast, Nussbaum seeks to define or specify "human ends across all areas of human life" and in so doing delineates a relatively "thick" conception of the human good.[17] Nussbaum argues that it is both possible and necessary for persons today to reach agreement on a "thick" understanding of the human good and she believes that doing so will facilitate social and political arrangements that will contribute to the flourishing of all persons.

Even while insisting that it is both possible and necessary to articulate a thick conception of the good in today's pluralistic world, Nussbaum nevertheless holds that this conception must be "vague," providing an "outline sketch of the good life" while admitting of "many concrete specifications."[18] This "sketch" of the good life provides enough guidance to be helpful and constructive while still leaving "a great deal of latitude . . . for citizens to specify each of the components more concretely, and with much variety, in their lives as they plan them."[19] It also helps the capabilities approach "have broad applicability to cross-cultural deliberations."[20]

In addition to allowing for flexible application of her theory across many different cultures and places, Nussbaum's vague conception of the good allows her to accommodate a changing conception of what the good means over time. This avoids the pitfall of getting locked into a past understanding of the good simply because it is "traditional" while ignoring the real reason the conception was developed in the first place: to facilitate human flourishing. What "human beings want and seek is not conformity with the past, it is the good. So our systems of law should make it possible for them to progress beyond the past, when they have agreed that a change is good."[21]

While rejecting certain aspects of Rawls's efforts to reconstruct an adequate theory of justice for the age in which we live, Nussbaum has made it clear that she believes her own account of the good could be supported along the lines described by Rawls as an "overlapping consensus."[22] What she understands Rawls to be doing is to put "forward something that people from many different traditions, with many different conceptions of the good, can agree on as the necessary basis for pursuing their good life." Like "Rawls's account of primary goods, this more comprehensive list of the good is proposed as the object of a specifically political consensus."[23] But where Rawls sought to produce this overlapping consensus by keeping his conception of the good a "thin" one, Nussbaum seeks to accomplish the same thing by articulating a comparatively thick description of the human good, but one "vague" enough to allow for specification across many different cultural and political settings.

The Essential Capabilities and Limitations of Human Life

Nussbaum identifies the essential human capabilities that give expression to her conception of the good human life through a three-stage argument. In the first stage she identifies what she understands to be the distinctive activities of the human person by asking questions like the following: "What are the characteristic activities of the human being? What does the human being do, characteristically, as such—and not, say, as a member of a particular group or particular local community?"[24] In other words, she wants to know "what are the forms of activity, of doing and being, that constitute the human form of life and distinguish it from other actual or imaginable forms of life, such as the lives of animals and plants, or, on the other hand, of immortal gods as imagined in myths and legends (which frequently have precisely the function of delimiting the human)?"[25] Consistent with her commitment to a revisable conception of the good, she emphasizes that the activities she lists in answer to these questions are only provisional, a starting point for conversation and debate; they are not put forward as the definitive list of human activities for all time. But she is equally clear that agreement can be reached on at least some sort of list that identifies essential activities of what constitutes a human life.

In the second stage she argues that the good human life will involve the ability to carry out these activities. If there are activities that are characteristically human, and one is unable to perform any one of them (for whatever reason), one is not living a life consistent with what it means to be a human being. This gives her a way to evaluate a person or society in relation to the good human life. The good life is one where these characteristic activities are "functional" in the person; the good society is one where its citizens have the functional capabilities she identifies. Nussbaum believes that this qualitative evaluative approach is a far more sensitive and sensible indicator of the well-being of a person or society than the more quantitative and typical measures of average income, gross national product, and so on.

In the third stage of her argument, Nussbaum reasons that, because the ability to perform these activities is endemic to a good human life, human beings who are unable to perform them have a claim on society. That claim can be a negative one, for example, a claim that society should remove impediments that block the performance of these activities in any of its citizens. Or it can be a positive one, that society must actively support institutions that enable the development in each of its citizens of those things necessary to execute the activities in question. In each case, Nussbaum sees the state as a primary actor in the distribution of the social resources necessary to accomplish this goal.

This link between human capabilities and the claims on society that follow from them makes Nussbaum's capabilities theory very much like a human rights theory and Nussbaum would not dispute this comparison. She is quite explicit that the items on the list she puts forward constitute "a ground-floor or minimal conception of the good" and in this way her essential conception of the human takes on "the role traditionally played in liberal political theory by a conception of the right." Like rights, the presence of at least a rudimentary capacity in the areas she describes "regulates the parameters of what can be chosen"—the mere presence of a capacity does not itself determine what course of action a person will take but simply makes possible a variety of courses of action.[26]

Nussbaum also stresses that, to the degree that her description of capabilities can be equated to rights, the rights in question are *human* rights. A human right is "a claim of an especially urgent and powerful sort, one that can be justified by an ethical argument that can command a broad cross-cultural consensus, and one that does not cease to be morally salient when circumstances render its recognition inefficient." A human right is one that "derives not from a person's particular situation of privilege or power or skill, but instead, just from the fact of being human."[27] On this point she aligns herself quite closely with the meaning of human rights in the Catholic social tradition.[28]

She makes one more important distinction, that between capabilities and limitations. Capabilities are those things which, by their presence or absence, allow one to judge whether the life in question is a good human life. The evaluation of these is straightforward—it is good that a capability is present and it is bad that a capability is absent. Limits of human life function differently than do capabilities. For example, it is normal to struggle against limitations—it would be odd if we did not wish to alleviate such things as pain and hunger. "On the other hand, we cannot assume that the correct evaluative conclusion to draw is that we should try as hard as possible to get rid of the limit altogether. It is characteristic of human life to prefer recurrent hunger plus eating to a life with neither hunger nor eating."[29] Yet one could not say the same thing about practical reason. Few would argue that it is a good thing to have recurrent deficits of practical reason; all things being equal people would like to be possessed of sound practical judgment as much as possible.

The capabilities that on Nussbaum's reading are "part of any life that we count as a human life" are shown in table 1.[30] In identifying the

Table 1. Capabilities for a Good Human Life

Life	"Being able to live to the end of a human life of normal length; not dying prematurely, or before one's life is so reduced as to be not worth living."
Bodily Health	"Being able to have good health, including reproductive health; to be adequately nourished; to have adequate shelter."
Bodily Integrity	"Being able to move freely from place to place; having one's bodily boundaries treated as sovereign, i.e. being able to be secure against violent assault, including sexual assault, child sexual abuse, and domestic violence; having opportunities for sexual satisfaction and for choice in matters of reproduction."
Senses, Imagination, and Thought	"Being able to use the senses, being able to imagine, think, and reason—and to do these things in a 'truly human' way, a way informed and cultivated by an adequate education, including, but by no means limited to, literacy and basic mathematical and scientific training. Being able to use imagination and thought in connection with experiencing and producing self-expressive works and events of one's own choice, religious, literary, musical, and so forth. Being able to use one's mind in ways protected by guarantees of freedom of expression with respect to both political and artistic speech, and freedom of religious exercise. Being able to search for the ultimate meaning of life in one's own way. Being able to have pleasurable experiences, and to avoid non-necessary pain."
Emotions	"Being able to have attachments to things and people outside ourselves; to love those who love and care for us, to grieve at their absence; in general, to love, to grieve, to experience longing, gratitude, and justified anger. Not having one's emotional development blighted by overwhelming anxiety, or by traumatic events of abuse or neglect. (Supporting this capability means supporting forms of human association that can be shown to be crucial in their development.)"
Practical Reason	"Being able to form a conception of the good and to engage in critical reflection about the planning of one's own life. (This entails protection for the liberty of conscience.)"
Affiliation	"A. Being able to live with and toward others, to recognize and show concern for other human beings, to engage in various forms of social interaction; to be able to imagine the situation of another and to have compassion for that situation; to have the capability for both justice and friendship. (Protecting this capability means protecting institutions that constitute and nourish such forms of affiliation, and also protecting the freedom of assembly and political speech.)"

Table 1. Capabilities for a Good Human Life (*cont.*)

	"B. Having the social bases of self-respect and non-humiliation; being able to be treated as a dignified being whose worth is equal to that of others. This entails, at a minimum, protections against discrimination on the basis of race, sex, sexual orientation, religion, caste, ethnicity, or national origin. In work, being able to work as a human being, exercising practical reason and entering into meaningful relationships of mutual recognition with others."
Other Species	"Being able to live with concern for and in relation to animals, plants, and the world of nature."
Play	"Being able to laugh, to play, to enjoy recreational activities."
Control over One's Environment	"A. Political. Being able to participate effectively in political choices that govern one's life; having the right of political participation, protections of free speech and association."
	"B. Material. Being able to hold property (both land and movable goods), not just formally but in terms of real opportunity; and having property rights on an equal basis with others; having the right to seek employment on an equal basis with others; having the freedom from unwarranted search and seizure."

essential capabilities, Nussbaum presents a vision of a good human life. A life that lacks any one of these capabilities or is unable to live within the prescribed limits, no matter what else it has, will fall short of being a good life. In Nussbaum's language, in order to have a good life, these basic capabilities and limits must be "functional." For example, Nussbaum lists bodily health as an essential capacity of being human. This means, among other things, that food, drink, and shelter are necessities. The functional capabilities that correspond to bodily health are "[b]eing able to have good health, including reproductive health; to be adequately nourished; to have adequate shelter."[31] Table 1 shows the correlation between each of the essentially human characteristics Nussbaum describes and their respective functional capabilities.

Nussbaum is emphatic that the good human life will have each of these functional capabilities and that a life that lacked any one of them will in that respect be diminished.[32] This means that one cannot try to make up for the absence of one capability (say, practical reason) by "doubling up" on another (say, control over one's environment). A minimal level of functioning for each capability must be present in order to live a good human life. On the other hand, Nussbaum does not believe that each functional capability is the equal of any other. "[T]wo . . . play a special role as architectonic, holding the whole enterprise together and making it human."[33] These two are practical reason and affiliation. These two capabilities "both organize and suffuse all the others, making their pursuit truly human."[34] For example, work without the exercise of practical reason and affiliation is not truly *human* work, it is on the order of a cog in a machine.

The fact that practical reason is so central to the human life is one reason why Nussbaum argues that public planning and legislation should aim not for actual functioning in persons but for the capability to function. This is why she precedes each functional capability with the phrase "being able to. . . ." Her aim is to give people the choice to perform certain functions, not to dictate that they must actually exercise these functions. And this means dedicating enough public resources to make such choices possible. This distinction between seeing the goal of public policy as enabling the *capability* to function rather than requiring the *actual functioning* makes Nussbaum's Aristotelianism "liberal" in its outlook. The emphasis on functional capabilities does not preclude the ability of individuals to make choices in accordance with their own conception of the good. So, for example, it is perfectly legitimate that religious (or any other) persons choose to fast, but there is a crucial difference between going hungry because of one's choice to fast and going hungry because one does not have access to adequate nutrition.[35]

There are additional parallels between Nussbaum's capabilities theory and liberal human rights theories. Rawls argues that sociability and practical reason are essential to human flourishing and therefore count as primary goods. Nussbaum also believes that Rawls's commitment to liberty, to social conditions that are conducive to self-respect, and to the idea of separateness of persons find corollaries in her own effort to delineate the basic shape of a human life.

There are also important differences between Nussbaum's approach and that of political liberals. For example, Rawls tends to evaluate the well-being of societies and persons by focusing on the distribution of resources and commodities. His famous "difference principle," which states that inequalities will be tolerated only when such inequalities will be to the benefit of the least advantaged, clearly has in mind disparities in income and wealth.[36] By contrast, for Nussbaum income and wealth, while not unimportant, should not be understood as "good in their own right; they are good only insofar as they promote human functioning."[37] She considers contemporary liberal approaches such as Rawls's to have difficulty dealing with the Marxist idea that "workers who lack control over their own activity and its products lead lives less than fully human, even if they do get adequate wages."[38] Meaningful work, and not just well-paying work, is integral to leading a full human life.

CAPABILITIES AND ASSETS

Nussbaum stresses that the development of the capabilities necessary for a life of human flourishing depends upon political and social institutions. These convictions are shared by those working on strategies and policies aimed at helping the poor to accumulate assets. As in the capabilities approach, the point or goal of asset building is ultimately the full development of human capacities.

The capabilities approach and the asset-building approach share, among other things, a dissatisfaction with certain methods for assessing the quality of life in a given society. The most prominent of the methods has been the use of aggregate economic data such as the Gross National Product. On this view, an increase in per capita GNP is equated with an increase in quality of life of society's members and countries with higher per capita GNP are seen to have a better quality of life than those with lower per capita GNP. Maximizing per capita GNP thus becomes the goal of development. Both Nussbaum and advocates of asset building object to such aggregate measures of human well-being and do so for similar reasons. First, *aggregate* measures of economic activity do not address the *distribution* of economic and social goods and because of this, obscure how each *individual* person within society is faring. Robust per capita GNP can occur at the same time that some in society experience substantial decreases in their quality of life. Likewise, countries with similar GNP per capita "can exhibit great distributional variations."[39]

Using aggregate economic data as a quality of life indicator is problematic for a second reason. As Nussbaum points out, such data does not convey whether important non-economic goods are also being realized. South Africa under an apartheid regime had a relatively high GNP per capita, for example. Likewise, there is wide variation with respect to gender equality among countries with similar GNP per capita. More generally, aggregate economic data does not capture whether or not the whole range of human capabilities identified earlier are being realized. For both capabilities theorists and those in the field of asset building, the abilities of each member of society to manifest important human capabilities is a much better quality of life indicator than are measures of aggregate economic activity.[40]

Capabilities, while not unrelated to economic well-being, clearly go far beyond this. Since Nussbaum's approach specifies a broad range of human capabilities for the purpose of evaluating the overall well-being of those within a given society, it is possible within her model to be extremely well-off financially while being impoverished on other important levels. The reverse is also true, at least in certain areas. Nussbaum argues, for example, that wealth and income "are not always well correlated" with important goods "such as life expectancy, infant mortality, educational opportunities, employment opportunities, political liberties, [and] the quality of race and gender relations."[41] Those in the asset-building field would dispute whether some of the items mentioned in her list are not well correlated with wealth, but they would agree with her that per capita GNP does not tell the whole story and that the distribution of financial and real assets is significant when it comes to human well-being. For her part, it is interesting and significant that Nussbaum revised her initial list of human capabilities so that it now recognizes the role that property rights can play in enabling full human functioning.[42] As she herself acknowledges, the inclusion of the right to hold property came from her experience with women in India who conveyed to her just how important property ownership was for their full inclusion in society and for determining their quality of life in general. As she puts it, "Everywhere I went [in India] . . . I heard women saying that having equal land rights . . . and having access to credit, are crucial determinants of their life quality."[43] A vivid illustration of this can be found in *Women and Human Development* in which she narrates the circumstances of Vasanti, a woman she met in India:

> The script of Vasanti's life has been largely written by men on whom she has been dependent: her father, her husband, the brothers who helped her out when her marriage collapsed. This dependency put

her at risk with respect to life and health, denied her the education that would have developed her powers of thought, and prevented her from thinking of herself as a person with a plan of life to shape and choices to make. In the marriage itself she fared worst of all, losing her bodily integrity to domestic violence, her emotional equanimity to fear, and being cut off from meaningful forms of affiliation, familial, friendly, and civic. For these reasons, she did not really have the conception of herself as a free and dignified being whose worth is equal to that of others. We should note that mundane matters of property, employment, and credit played a large role here: the fact that she held no property in her own name, had no literacy and no employment-related skills, and no access to credit except from male relatives, all this cemented her dependent status and kept her in an abusive relationship far longer than would otherwise have been her wish.[44]

This narrative illustrates how interrelated and interconnected the capabilities are to one another, and "how the absence of one, bad in itself, also erodes others."[45] Thus it becomes apparent that facilitating asset building for the poor will not in itself solve all of the problems faced by the poor, but it seems equally clear that social policy cannot continue to ignore asset building for the poor, given the integral role it can play in enabling self-efficacy.

Michael Sherraden comes to a similar conclusion on the basis of similar encounters. He reports that his idea of asset building for the poor emerged out of discussions that he had with women who live in poverty in the United States. Like Nussbaum, Sherraden emphasizes the importance of an inductive approach in addressing issues that are faced by the poor. He underscores that this is especially important for those working on policy in part because "policy thinking will be much better if it is from the ground up, based in the realities of people's lives. . . . There is enormous expertise in the target population and . . . [it is] a huge mistake . . . [to] ignore this expertise."[46] The inductive approach is appropriate not only for measuring economic health, but it also should affect how public policy is formulated and implemented. If well-being is conceptualized in terms of capabilities rather than income and consumption, social policies would take a different form as well. What asset building brings is a policy approach that supports the development of a variety of capacities. One strength of the asset-building model is that it provides a particular pathway along which to actualize a range of basic and fundamental human capabilities and it recognizes that the income-consumption approach is necessary but not sufficient for this task.

Sometimes there is clear and obvious overlap between the capabilities that Nussbaum enumerates and those of the asset-building approach; at other times the connections between these two approaches is less clear. In order to see more clearly how an asset-building approach is related to the capabilities approach, it will be helpful to specify more precisely the positive psychological, familial, social, and political effects that are enabled by asset building. Empirical research on the positive effects of asset holding suggests that assets are correlated with a wide range of capabilities and/or that they create conditions favorable to the development of capabilities. While there is an implied relationship between the known positive effects of asset holding and the development or actualization of the capabilities that Nussbaum identifies, there is no one-to-one correlation between Nussbaum's capabilities and those associated with economic assets. The positive effects of assets have already been alluded to in chapter one; however, it will be helpful to expand upon them more fully here.

An important role played by assets is to protect individuals or families from the effects of disruptions in the flow of income. Here, there is a convergence with Nussbaum's categories of bodily integrity and control over one's environment. These disruptions may be caused by deterioration of macroeconomic conditions, such as a severe recession. They can also be caused by events that have discreet effects upon individuals or their families, such as the death or illness of a primary breadwinner, or serious illness of a child not covered by insurance, or marital break-up. Each of these scenarios creates severe stress on families. A substantial body of research suggests that this stress is mitigated by the presence of assets. Such families, when faced with these conditions, are "more likely to maintain social and economic equilibrium until sufficient income can be reestablished."[47] By contrast, families who are asset poor and thus more vulnerable to economic worries are "more likely to bear the wounds of mental depression, rage, marital breakup, child and spouse abuse, alcohol and drug use, and so forth."[48] These stressors are felt all the more acutely in contexts where social support during economic shocks is minimal or absent. For example, the stress on individuals and families is likely to be more severe in countries that lack robust economic support for those who lose their job and the associated benefits such as health care. In sum, assets can be an important contributor to household stability.

If the absence of sufficient assets leaves individuals and families more vulnerable to a variety of stressors, the presence of assets is correlated with a range of positive effects on human well-being. Assets are associated with the promotion of human capital along a variety of fronts. There is a strong correlation between assets and educational attainment. Nussbaum, Amartya Sen, and other capability theorists argue that personal economic development is facilitated by the development of human capital. That is, economic development begins with "education, learning, and skill formation" which, in turn, help people to become "much more productive over time, and this contributes greatly to the process of economic expansion."[49] However, asset-building theorists argue that, in practice, this process can happen in reverse. That is, "tangible assets also stimulate people to improve themselves."[50] Those who have assets are more likely to take an interest in and learn about financial matters. In so doing, they become actively involved in an important educational process that has ongoing significance for their economic well-being. There is evidence that this involvement "leads to increased income and accumulation of assets."[51] Those who own homes are no doubt familiar with the phrase "sweat equity." This term describes the fact that those who own their home are more likely to invest their time and money in improving that home, which in turn increases the value of the home. This phenomenon has important implications for public policy, particularly one aimed at helping persons to accumulate assets. When those without assets are provided with the institutional and material means to accumulate assets, it is likely that these same persons will become much more interested in learning about asset accumulation and acquainting themselves with the means to enhance the value of those assets.

Related to the idea that assets promote human capital is the notion that assets promote focus and specialization, which is one example of what Martha Nussbaum means by practical reason. Sherraden notes that this phenomenon was observed as far back as 1776 in Adam Smith's *An Inquiry into the Nature and Causes of Wealth of Nations*. For example, Smith notes that "a weaver cannot apply himself entirely to his peculiar business, unless there is beforehand stored up somewhere . . . a stock sufficient to maintain him, and to supply him with the materials and tools of his work. . . . This accumulation must, evidently, be previous to his applying his industry for so long a time to such a peculiar business."[52] Focus and specialization are associated with greater net worth. Even when members of poor households wish to specialize, their time and energy is frequently taken up by short-term and odd jobs that are unrelated to the discipline or task in which they wish to specialize. Sherraden notes two reasons for this: first, that "assets are needed in advance of income flows to purchase the tools and skills for specialization. Second, without assets, there are no resources to pay others for required goods and services while one specializes."[53] A person with no resources is, of necessity, pressed into becoming a "jack of all trades" in order to deal with the inevitable things that break down in life. This reality diminishes the time and energy available to give to specialization.

Assets are also associated with greater tolerance for risk taking and increased personal efficacy. This behavioral effect illustrates the necessity of taking into account the effect of assets that is not entirely economic, but also psychological. Here, there is a convergence with Nussbaum's category of senses, imagination, and thought as well as practical reason and the capacity to plan one's life. Many economic models limit the utility of assets to purchasing power. However, there is a developing body of literature that recognizes the psychological and behavioral effects of owning assets. Assets can enable one to have a worldview or hold a vision for oneself that is sustaining long before ever actualizing that vision. Schreiner and Sherraden note that even "the mere thought of the opportunities enabled by the ownership of savings provides benefits to the saver, even if none of these opportunities are ever realized. In the economic model, in contrast, assets matter only in use. In the psychological model, ownership itself, regardless of use, also matters, because people look ahead and enjoy contemplating the possible economic effects of the use of their savings."[54] These beneficial psychological effects of assets can enhance a sense of personal efficacy and agency that may also lead individuals to take positive risks that move one out of one's comfort zone and expand one's horizons.

For better or worse, another effect of assets is that they can increase social influence and enhance the position one holds in certain social interactions. This has resonance with Nussbaum's categories of affiliation and control over one's environment. Those who hold assets are much more likely to have access to social networks that contribute to and sustain their superior economic status. These networks provide access to privileged information, such as job openings, investment opportunities, funding sources, and so on. The wealthy also tend to have greater access to those who make policy and thus can influence these decisionmakers in ways that the poor cannot. Perhaps one of the most important effects of wealth in social interactions is the freedom from coercion it provides when negotiating with others. Those with wealth are in a much better position to object to unfair labor practices including inadequate salary and unjust working conditions and have more freedom to leave an unsatisfactory work environment.[55]

Another important feature of asset ownership is its correlation with political participation. Here again are connections with Nussbaum's categories of affiliation and control over one's environment. There is considerable data that show a strong relationship between ownership and political activity. As Sherraden observes, those who have assets have both "greater incentives and greater resources to participate in the political process." Homeowners are more likely to vote, and home ownership has been shown to contribute to political stability.[56] Commenting on this feature of asset ownership, the Organization for Economic Cooperation and Development (OECD) writes that with "assets to protect, people pay attention to where their leaders lead them. They can no longer afford to live in 'exclusion'. . . . They join the system. This increases social cohesion."[57] There is evidence that assets also increase local political involvement and inspire people to become more actively involved in their local communities because they have a greater stake in them. In short, asset ownership encourages social and political participation. Those who are not owners tend to be marginalized not only economically, but politically and socially as well. To the extent that democracies and the common good depend upon widespread participation of all members of a society, both would seem to benefit from increasing asset ownership.

These are not new ideas. As Michael Lind points out, among democratic traditions, there is a long history of recognizing a relationship between ownership and political participation.[58] In these traditions, widespread ownership is understood to be essential to effective democratic governance. Lind quotes John Adams's argument in 1776 that since "power always follows property" a vibrant democracy would "make the acquisition of land easy to every member of society," and similarly, Ezra Stiles, "We may as well think to repeal the great laws of attraction and gravitation, as to think of continuing a popular government without a good degree of equality among the people as to their property."[59] Another quote is from Thomas Hart Benton:

> The basis of a democratic and a republican form of government is, a fundamental law, favoring an equal or rather a general distribution of property. It is not necessary nor possible that every citizen should have exactly an equal portion of land and goods, but the [inheritance] laws of such a state should require an equal distribution of intestate estates, and bar all perpetuities.[60]

And in the twentieth century, Lind reports that Franklin Roosevelt emphasized that "[a]ny elemental policy, economic or political, which tends . . . to concentrate control in the hands of a few small, powerful groups, is directly opposed to the stability of government and to democratic government itself."[61]

Assets have also been shown to have important intergenerational welfare effects. Here, the connections with Nussbaum are linked to bodily health, practical reason, and emotional development, among others. Children born to families with sufficient assets benefit in a myriad of ways. They have been shown to have better nutrition, health, education, and so on. In addition, assets "decrease the risk of intergenerational poverty transmission."[62] This phenomenon has to do with the distinctive quality of wealth when compared to income. No matter what level of earned income parents receive, they cannot bequeath that income to their children. Assets, on the other hand, can be passed on to one's offspring. This observation is a significant one in considering the enormous disparities in wealth between, for example, white Americans and African Americans. These disparities cannot be explained by differences in income alone (which are, nevertheless, significant), but are the result of past and present discrimination in asset-building policies at the federal, state, and local levels.[63] The cumulative nature of wealth accumulation means that asset denial at any point in history tends to have a cumulative effect on subsequent generations. Asset-denial initiatives directed at African Americans have been a central aspect of American life from the very beginning and continue in less blatant forms into the present moment.[64]

One of the most important features of assets is that they can help orient persons toward the future. Here is a convergence with Nussbaum's category of practical reason where she includes the notion of "being able to engage in critical reflection about the planning of one's . . . life."[65] Assets are inherently long term. As Sherraden observes, "They financially connect the present with the future. Indeed, in a sense, assets *are* the future. They are hope in concrete form. . . . If people are to believe in a viable future, there must be some tangible link between now and then. In very many situations, assets are that link."[66] Absent the hope of a better economic future, and given the pressing demands of the present simply to survive, it is understandable that those who are poor would focus primarily on the present. However, when even the hope of assets is present, one can observe a substantial psychological and behavioral benefit. One such example was observed in the early 1980s when Eugene Lang, a multimillionaire, offered college tuition to a group of sixth graders in Harlem. Lang told them that if they graduated from high school he would pay their college tuition. The high school drop-out rate in this part of Harlem was between 50 and 75 percent, and almost none of those who graduated went on to college. Among the group that Lang spoke to, all who remained in the New York area stayed in high school and nearly all of them graduated. In 1988, approximately half of those students who had graduated from high school were enrolled in college.[67] An important aspect of this example is that it disentangles the effects of asset ownership from the effects of their use. Because in this example the asset—the college tuition—is not used until students enrolled in college, it is easier to attribute the positive effects to asset ownership, rather than to their use. Schreiner and Sherraden point out that "[t]hese are purely socio-psychological effects of asset ownership, not economic effects of asset use."[68] The observation that the presence of assets has important psychological and behavioral effects long before their use has important implications for public policy. Policymakers who are interested in not only alleviating the immediate effects of poverty but also in shaping the psychological outlook and behaviors of the poor should be especially supportive of efforts to help the poor accumulate assets.

In summary, taken together, these and other benefits of the asset-building approach suggest that asset building offers a distinctive and

complementary approach to traditional income-based poverty alleviation policies and offers a concrete way in which society can promote
the kind of capabilities that lead to human flourishing and the stability
of society. Just as Nussbaum adds particularity to the norms of Catholic
social thought, so do the empirical effects of asset building outlined in
the research suggest concrete ways in which Nussbaum's "thick, vague"
notions of flourishing can be developed.

Similar to Nussbaum, asset-based policy is less focused on meeting
the short-term needs of the poor and instead focuses on the long-term
development of individuals. As Michael Sherraden puts it:

> Asset-based policy is not primarily about problem amelioration or
> fighting poverty. It is about enabling individuals and families to be
> in control of their lives, develop capabilities, and contribute to soci-
> ety and the economy. While this will involve tackling poverty, we
> should remember that the central goal of asset-based policies is de-
> velopment in a broader context. It is about building the capacity of
> people with low incomes and allowing them to seek opportunities.[69]

Like the capability approach, asset-building strategies recognize
the importance of institutional and social supports as integral to ac-
complishing the intended goal. Asset building can be seen as *a* way to
operationalize in policy what the capability approach endorses. While
there is no one-to-one correlation between Nussbaum's capabilities
and those correlated with economic assets, there is an implied relationship between the known positive effects of asset holding and the development or actualization of the capabilities that Nussbaum identifies.
Both Nussbaum and Amartya Sen associate the actualization of capabilities with human freedom. The benefits of asset building can certainly be described as freedom enhancing. The ability to withstand
economic shocks, to secure adequate housing, to provide a stable
household environment for one's children, to benefit from educational
attainment, to be able to devote one's time and energy to one's chosen
vocation or specialty, to have the security to take risks for those things
which one values, to be able to resist unjust demands by one's employer,
and so on, is a way of describing dimensions of human freedom.

CHAPTER FOUR

Asset Discrimination

Racism is not merely one sin among many; it is a radical evil that divides the human family and denies the new creation of a redeemed world. To struggle against it demands an equally radical transformation, in our own minds and hearts as well as in the structure of our society.

—U.S. Catholic Bishops

From the very beginning, the Church's social teachings have rejected the idea that optimal economic conditions will be obtained so long as the market is left to its own devices; economies are not governed by impersonal and unalterable laws but are, rather, human institutions which need to be subordinated to the good of all. This observation is clearly borne out by human history, which has shown that when persons are excluded or denied opportunities to accumulate assets that are provided to others, the result is decreased standard of living, social unrest, political disenfranchisement, and a general lack of opportunity to develop human resources. This has ramifications for the whole society, or what Catholic social thought would call the common good. When those who are poor are not able to contribute to society to the best of their ability, all suffer. When those who are wealthy come to see the generation and protection of their wealth as the end of all economic activity, not only does society suffer but those who are materially wealthy are impoverished in significant ways.

The recognition that human beings are material and spiritual, individual and social, necessarily means that a life spent solely in pursuit of personal material gain is an impoverished life, incapable of providing authentic human happiness. What is called for is not ascetic denial but a life of moderation coupled to a deep commitment to justice for all persons. Important measures of economic justice include whether or not the economy meets all persons' basic needs, provides to all the opportunity to participate in the economic life of society, and does so in a way that honors human dignity and contributes to the common good. As we have seen, the social teachings of the Church argue that expanding ownership to all is an important means for achieving each of these aims.

Both the capabilities approach and Catholic social thought recognize that human beings are historical beings and they become who they are within a particular historical context. It is one thing to assert that the development of human capabilities is central to the realization of human dignity; it is another thing to recognize the long history of impediments to their development. These impediments must be removed and positive steps taken if all of those in society are to be enabled to develop to their full potential. It is one thing to recognize that all human beings are created in the image of God and therefore have an inherent dignity; it is another thing altogether to recognize the historical denial of this claim and its impact on any particular individual or whole groups of peoples. Efforts to denigrate persons because of their race, class, ethnicity, or gender have had, and continue to have, devastating personal, social, political, and economic effects.

President Obama summarized the history of asset discrimination in the United States:

> We do not need to recite here the history of racial injustice in this country. But we do need to remind ourselves that so many of the disparities that exist in the African-American community today can be directly traced to inequalities passed on from an earlier generation that suffered under the brutal legacy of slavery and Jim Crow. . . . Legalized discrimination—where blacks were prevented, often through violence, from owning property, or loans were not granted to African-American business owners, or black homeowners could not access FHA mortgages, or blacks were excluded from unions, or the police force, or fire departments—meant that black families

could not amass any meaningful wealth to bequeath to future generations. That history helps explain the wealth and income gap between black and white, and the concentrated pockets of poverty that
persists in so many of today's urban and rural communities.[1]

This history offers an explanation for the current disparities in
wealth between whites and blacks and illuminates what must be done
going forward if those who are today lacking in wealth are to be given
the opportunity to accumulate wealth. Many studies have documented
the existence of a substantial wealth gap between white and black Americans that is significantly larger than, and not explained by, differences
in income.[2] The disparity between white and black wealth can be explained, at least in part, by particular public policies that favored wealth
accumulation for white Americans while denying these same opportunities to African Americans. This history of discrimination demonstrates that public policies do significantly impact persons' ability to
accumulate wealth. The sharp differences between the economic opportunities of white and black Americans is emblematic of what can
happen to any group of people that is systematically excluded from programs that contribute to economic prosperity and human well-being.

ASSET DISCRIMINATION IN U.S. HISTORY

The United States has a long history of asset discrimination and asset denial, one obscured all too easily by the seductive claim that the United
States is a land of endless opportunity, especially for those who are willing
to work hard and 'play by the rules.' The so-called 'rules' have not been
applied equally to all persons and any fair-minded view of U.S. history
would have to include the judgment that asset denial to select groups of
people has played an integral role in the United States from its inception.
The forceful removal and re-appropriation of the land of Native Americans by the colonizers from Europe, the redistribution of the income and
wealth from the labor of African slaves to their white 'owners', the thwart-
ing of policies aimed at expanding ownership to all in the period following the Civil War, the deliberate exclusion of some (mostly African
Americans) from Depression-era initiatives intended to protect and promote property ownership, the use of restrictive covenants to maintain

white monopolies on rapidly appreciating housing, and the practice of red-lining by banks and other mortgage lenders are all part of this history.

The Era of Reconstruction: A Missed Opportunity

While public policies have helped to facilitate asset accumulation for many Americans, access to the benefits of these policies has often been limited on the basis of race. During and just after the end of the American Civil War, in the period commonly referred to as the Era of Reconstruction, it appeared that things might be otherwise.

The Homestead Act of 1862, signed into law by Abraham Lincoln on May 20 of that year, signaled the federal government's intention to distribute land to persons who were not yet landowners. It is now widely acknowledged that this act helped shape the settlement of land in the United States well into the twentieth century. Over the life of this act, some "287.5 million acres of the public domain were granted or sold to homesteaders." This figure represents approximately "20 percent of public land and is comparable to the amount of land granted to states and the acreage sold or awarded to railroads and other corporate interests."[3]

The Homestead Act of 1862 embodied in law a growing consensus "concerning the rights of citizenship, how the nation's land resources would be managed, and whether an opportunity should be provided for individuals other than the wealthy to own property. . . ."[4] The act provided that U.S. citizens, or those who had filed for citizenship, "heads of household, military veterans, and those over 21 years of age were entitled to 160 acres of unappropriated land as long as they had not borne arms against the U.S. government."[5] (Blacks could not apply for homesteads until the passage of the Southern Homestead Act in 1866.) Those interested in obtaining land were required to file an application, swear that the property was for one's own use, and live on the land for at least five years. After five years, the applicant would be granted title to the land after providing evidence that the occupancy conditions had been met and "paying nominal charges to the appropriate land office."[6] As "one of the nation's first major domestic policies," the Homestead Act was a significant asset-building initiative.[7] "Citizens with few or no assets could find an unoccupied 160 acres, file a homestead application and, after living on the land for five years, possess crops, land, and financial independence. In a sense, the government was not only giving away land, but also the opportunity for upward mobility and a more secure future for oneself and one's children."[8]

Beginning with the Emancipation Proclamation, accelerating with the cumulative victories of the Northern armies over the South, and culminating with the ratification of the Thirteenth Amendment to the U.S. Constitution, some four million former slaves were freed. The vast majority of the 'freedmen', as the former slaves would be called, were without property.[9] President Lincoln issued the Emancipation Proclamation stating, in part, "That on the first day of January, in the year of our Lord one thousand eight hundred and sixty-three, all persons held as slaves within any State or designated part of a State, the people whereof shall then be in rebellion against the United States, shall be then, thenceforward, and forever free; and the Executive Government of the United States, including the military and naval authority thereof, will recognize and maintain the freedom of such persons, and will do no act or acts to repress such persons, or any of them, in any efforts they may make for their actual freedom."[10] The Thirteenth Amendment, ratified on December 18, 1865 by twenty-seven of the thirty-six states, stipulates that "[n]either slavery nor involuntary servitude, except as punishment for crime whereof the party shall have been duly convicted, shall exist within the United States, or any place subject to their jurisdiction." And that "Congress shall have power to enforce this article by appropriate legislation."

Despite congressional support and the support of President Lincoln, the extension of land ownership rights to African Americans was resisted by many Americans, not the least of which was the man who succeeded Lincoln after his assassination, Andrew Johnson. Congressional action, with the support of President Lincoln, had made it possible for former slaves to begin settling and farming land, some of which came from the land of their former masters, which was confiscated during the Civil War. Lincoln and his congressional allies clearly believed that the freedom of former slaves could not be secured in any permanent way without also providing them with ownership of land and, through this, the means to a reliable and stable source of income. When Lincoln was assassinated and President Johnson succeeded him, white Southerners found they now had a much more sympathetic executive willing to use his power in ways that were far more favorable to their personal interests. Johnson not only extended amnesty to those white

Southerners who had participated in the war, he also restored their property rights, returning to them the plantations and other land they had once owned. Where newly freed slaves had already settled such land, Johnson's actions took away from the latter what had been theirs.[11]

The connection between actual freedom and land ownership was not lost on the freedmen, as illustrated by the following letter by three freedmen—Henry Bram, Ishmael Moultrie, and Yates Sampson—to General Oliver Howard, the head of the Freedmen's Bureau, a government agency charged with the responsibility of caring for the needs of the newly freed slaves. These freedmen clearly understood that President Johnson's actions stripping them of the land that they had settled undermined their newly acquired freedom and threatened to return them to a state of slavery from which they had just been released:

> We were promised Homesteads by the government. If it does not carry out the promises Its agents made to us . . . we are left in a more unpleasant condition than our former. We are at the mercy of those who are combined to prevent us from getting land enough to lay our Fathers['] bones upon. We have property in Homes, horses, cattle, carriages, & articles of furniture; but we are landless and Homeless. . . . We cannot resist . . . Without being driven out Homeless upon the road.
>
> You will see that this is not the condition of really free men. You ask us to forgive the landowners of our Island. *You* only lost your right arm In the war and might forgive them. The man who tied me to a tree and gave me 39 lashes[;] who stripped and flogged my mother & sister & who will not let me stay in his empty hut except [unless] I will do His planting & be satisfied with His price & who combines with others to keep away land from me, well knowing I would not Have anything to do with Him If I had land of my own— that man, I cannot well forgive. Does it look as if he has forgiven me . . . [since] he tries to keep me in a condition of Helplessness.
>
> General, we cannot remain Here . . . [under] such condition[s] and if the government permits them to come back we ask it to help us to reach land where we shall not be slaves nor compelled to work for those who would treat us as such.[12]

These same freedmen also appealed their case to President Johnson:

This is our home. We have made These lands what they are. We were the only true and Loyal people that were found in possession of Lands. We have been always ready to strike for Liberty and humanity, yea to fight if need be To preserve this glorious Union. Shall not we who Are freedman [*sic*] and have been always true to this Union have the same rights as are enjoyed by Others? Have we broken any laws of these United States? Have we forfeited our rights of property In land—If not[,] then, are not our rights as A free people and good citizens of these United States To be considered before the rights of those who were Found in rebellion against this good and just government[?] ... If [the] Government does not make some provision by which we as Freedmen can obtain [a] Homestead, we have Not bettered our condition. ... We are ready to pay for this land When [the] Government calls for it. And now after What has been done will the good and just government take from us as this right and make us Subject to the will of those who cheated and Oppressed us for many years[?] God forbid! We the freedmen of this Island and of the state of South Carolina—

Do therefore petition to you as the President of these United States, that some provisions be made by which Every colored man can purchase and Hold it as his own. We wish to have [a] home, if it be but a few acres. ... We therefore look to you ... for protection and Equal Rights, with the privilege of Purchasing [a] Homestead right here in the Heart of South Carolina.[13]

These petitions contain themes that were widely shared by the freedmen. Among them is the recognition that their quality of life was closely linked to the ownership of property— "If the government does not make some provision by which we as freedmen can obtain a homestead, we have not bettered our condition." Furthermore, access to the land enabled them to generate the money needed to purchase the land and they were more than willing to do so. They recognize and elegantly articulate the manifest injustice facing them: having labored without pay for years and fought on behalf of the Union, they were now being stripped of the land in favor of those who had fought against the Union and enslaved them.[14]

In response to Johnson's move to restore land ownership to white Southerners and to deny ownership to blacks who had already settled and worked the land, Lyman Trumbull, a Republican representative from Pennsylvania, sponsored a bill that would have provided "three million acres for allotment to freedmen in parcels not exceeding forty acres." In addition, the bill would have ensured each "settler would be furnished a house and the necessary provisions for farming, such as mules, seed, and tools."[15] The Trumbull bill expressed legislatively what had already become a kind of mantra among the newly freed slaves, namely, that they would be provided "forty acres and a mule." The origins of this slogan are not entirely clear, but Oubre suggests they may be related to General William Tecumseh Sherman's postwar actions aimed at providing freed slaves with both property and the means to cultivate this property.[16] Sherman ordered that land be set aside in South Carolina for this purpose and provided the freed slaves with the equipment and animals needed to till the land.[17] However, President Johnson vetoed the Trumbull bill. An outraged Congress acted swiftly to pass another bill with a veto proof majority. That bill, passed in July 1866, was known as the Southern Homestead Act.[18]

The Southern Homestead Act made 46 million acres of public land available for sale in Alabama, Arkansas, Florida, Louisiana, and Mississippi.[19] The act, which was ultimately rescinded in 1876, limited purchases to relatively small parcels of land (80 and 160 acres) while explicitly prohibiting purchases by "speculators or those with mining and timber interests."[20] By limiting the power of wealthy individuals and corporations to accumulate large tracts of land, policymakers sought to make it possible for those without property, including freed slaves, to acquire it. The prospect of these new freedmen becoming owners of income-generating property was characterized by W. E. B. Du Bois as "America's chance to be a modern democracy."[21]

The Southern Homestead Act distributed land to whites and blacks alike. However, the mechanism by which the land was distributed was not the same for blacks and whites. Whites were able to purchase land directly with the help of low interest loans from banks. Blacks, by contrast, acquired their land through a government agency known as the Freedmen's Bureau. The Freedmen's Bureau, under the direction of General Oliver Howard, placed many restrictions on ownership of land by newly freed slaves. For example, Howard, seemingly oblivious to the fact that slaves and their forbearers had already worked the land without compensation for over two centuries, believed that newly freed slaves should not simply be gifted with land but rather should "earn" it. Because of this, Howard "recommended that northerners, including bureau agents, purchase or lease farms to provide work for the freedmen."[22] As a result, not only did white Northerners end up owning the greatest number of confiscated plantations but the majority of freedmen were ultimately unable to acquire land of their own. Howard's policy helped produce the sharecropper system that dominated the South after the Civil War. Sharecroppers were provided housing, seed, and other provisions in exchange for cultivating the land. They did not own the land or any of the instruments of production and were therefore dependent upon the white landlords who ensured that their tenants lived at a subsistence level.[23] In effect, the freedmen/sharecroppers were slaves under a different name.

The Freedmen's Bureau was also closely affiliated with the Freedmen's Savings and Trust Company, an institution created by Congress at the same time it created the bureau (1865).[24] The Freedmen's Bank, as it came to be known, was specifically created to accept deposits from blacks. This bank, which offered the promise of savings and wealth creation for many black Americans during this period, was necessary because nearly all Southern banks refused to accept deposits from the freedmen. Within five years of the founding of the bank, freedmen had deposited nearly 17 million dollars, and by July 1872, this savings had grown to over 31 million dollars.[25] However, after accepting deposits for nearly a decade, the bank failed in 1874 mostly as a result of "[h]ighly questionable no-interest loans from the bank to white companies," loans dispersed at the behest of the bank's white-controlled board of directors.[26] Understandably, the collapse of the Freedmen's Bank left many blacks distrustful of financial institutions. Writing thirty years after the crash of the Freedmen's Bank, W. E. B. Du Bois remarked,

> Then in one sad day came the crash,—all the hard-earned dollars of the freedmen disappeared; but that was the least of the loss,—all the faith in saving went too, and much of the faith in men; and that was a loss that a Nation which to-day sneers at Negro shiftlessness has never yet made good. Not even ten additional years of slavery could have done so much to throttle the thrift of the freedmen as the mismanagement and bankruptcy of the series of savings banks chartered by the Nation for their especial aid.[27]

The undermining of wealth accumulation by blacks was not limited to the collapse of the Freedmen's Bank or to the discrimination embedded in the Homestead Act. Blacks who managed to find the resources to leave the South and head west to pursue the promise offered by land grants there were often able to secure land ownership only to find later that their ownership status was not legally protected in many states. Dalton Conley notes that a "white person could come and lay legal claim to the land that a black individual had already settled, and the white person's title would be honored over that of the African American."[28]

The combined effect of these policies and practices was to dramatically limit the ownership and savings of the freed slaves and their families. Of the 1.5 million families which received land under the Homestead Act and Southern Homestead Act, only 5,500 of the new homesteads were owned by black families.[29]

The 'New Deal': Increasing Wealth for Whites, Asset Denial for Blacks

"No more critical situation ever faced the Negroes of America than that of today—not in 1830, nor in 1861, nor in 1867. More than ever the appeal of the Negro for the elementary justice falls on deaf ears. Three-fourths of us are disenfranchised; yet no writer on democratic reform says a word about Negroes."[30] It would surprise many Americans that W. E. B. Du Bois rendered this judgment in 1935. Discrimination against African Americans did not end despite Lincoln's proclamation nor with the effort by congressional majorities to provide economic security to freed slaves through the Southern Homestead Act. Indeed, discriminatory practices—in both the public and private sector—continued throughout the twentieth century. Even during times of great economic distress for all Americans, African Americans were systematically excluded from the welfare benefits provided to the majority of white Americans. This was especially true during the period in which Du Bois was writing—the Great Depression and the accompanying public policies aimed at righting the floundering U.S. economy. Many of these policies were characterized as protecting the asset holdings of ordinary Americans while also extending their ability to accumulate assets in the future. At every turn, African Americans were denied access to the benefits being provided to white Americans, *as a matter of public policy*. Du Bois recognized the debilitating effect that such actions would have on African Americans as a whole, widening the already dramatic inequalities between whites and blacks.

Discriminatory practices were embedded in several significant Depression-era policies and practices, including the distribution of Social Security benefits, eligibility requirements for home loans provided by the Home Owner's Loan Corporation (HOLC) and the Federal Housing Authority (FHA), Aid to Families with Dependent Children (AFDC), and the G.I. Bill.

The twentieth century marked a great expansion of government initiatives whose purpose was to provide Americans with greater financial security. Such initiatives became necessary especially during the crisis brought on by the stock market crash of 1929 and the subsequent worldwide economic depression. Through a series of dramatic legislative initiatives, the federal government sought to protect the value of Americans' dwindling assets, supplement the income of older and more vulnerable citizens, and, generally speaking, create a more positive and more secure sense of the country's future financial prospects. Almost all of these Depression-era initiatives continue to this day. What few Americans realize is that many of these programs were intentionally discriminatory and had they not been so would never have become law.

Perhaps the most widely known and appreciated legislative accomplishment of the Depression-era initiatives is the Social Security Act of 1935. One aspect of this act was the Old Age Insurance program, which while offering millions of Americans some modest financial security during retirement, "virtually excluded African Americans and Latinos" from its benefits.[31] It did this by exempting "agricultural and domestic workers from coverage." These exclusions were deemed necessary in order to gain support from Southern congressmen. Since African Americans were disproportionately represented in these job categories, they were disproportionately excluded from the benefits of Social Security. Indeed, earnings qualifications were set high enough so that "42 percent of black workers in occupations covered by social insurance did not earn enough to qualify for benefits compared to 22 percent for whites."[32] Moreover, because Social Security contributions cease above a certain income level, low-wage workers pay a higher proportion of their income to Social Security while receiving comparatively lower benefits. Additionally, because African Americans have on average a shorter life span, they receive retirement benefits from Social Security for a shorter period of time.[33] Although recent changes in the Social Security laws do include the kinds of work and income levels that were originally excluded, the effects of this initial exclusion continue to be felt. The generation of low-paid and agricultural and domestic workers denied Social Security benefits were unable to conserve an amount of savings equal to that benefit and, as a result, had nothing to pass on to their offspring.

Two other Depression-era federal initiatives have had a differential impact on asset accumulation between whites and blacks: the Home Owner's Loan Corporation (HOLC) and the Federal Housing Authority (FHA). The HOLC, founded in 1933, was established to assist home-owners at risk of default during the Great Depression. This agency systematically and explicitly incorporated "the evaluation of the racial composition or potential racial composition of the community" into their judgments of the creditworthiness of loan applicants.[34] Applicants residing in homes located within black or "mixed" neighborhoods were automatically judged to be high risk, thus ensuring that those living in these neighborhoods would not receive assistance from the HOLC. In fact, it is because of the practices of the HOLC that the current practice of discriminatory lending by private banks is known as "red-lining." The HOLC developed maps that assigned "various colors on a map ranging from green for the most desirable" (i.e., new construction, all-white neighborhoods) to red for the least desirable (i.e., racially mixed or all-black areas) and then used those maps in its judgment of the creditworthiness of loan applicants.[35]

The Federal Housing Authority, established in 1934, "ushered in the modern mortgage system that enabled people to buy homes on small down payments and at reasonable interest rates, with lengthy repayment periods and full loan amortization."[36] Prior to the formation of the FHA, most homeowners were required to make a down payment of at least 50 percent of the home's value and the terms of the loan were usually no longer than five years. "As a result, mortgages were available only to those with considerable wealth and income."[37]

While the FHA's loan program was remarkably successful in expanding homeownership to those of modest means, it engaged in loan practices whose purpose was to ensure the segregation of neighborhoods by race and class. According to the FHA's *Underwriting Manual*, "if a neighborhood is to retain stability, it is necessary that properties shall continue to be occupied by the same social and racial classes. A change in social or racial occupancy generally leads to instability and a reduction in values."[38] The manual recommended that "neighborhood stability" could best be ensured by "deed restrictions" in order to "supplement [local] zoning ordinances." Among the recommended deed restrictions we find "[p]rohibition of the occupancy of properties except by the race for which they were intended."[39] Such segregation was believed to be necessary in order to protect the value of the home and thereby protect the value of the loan. The FHA "was legally sanctioned to segregate Whites and Blacks" until the Supreme Court prohibited it in 1949.[40] The effect of that segregation policy was to place white Americans in homes and neighborhoods that produced substantial returns on their housing investment, while relegating black Americans to substandard homes and neighborhoods with much lower rates of housing appreciation.

This federal endorsement of segregation was accompanied by tactics and strategies at the local level, reinforced by, among other things, organized neighborhood associations whose purpose was to ensure that white neighborhoods remained white. These associations employed a number of different strategies to achieve this goal including: lobbying for zoning restrictions aimed at preventing blacks from living in a particular neighborhood; threatening to boycott businesses, including real estate agencies, that provided goods and services to blacks; purchasing the homes of black property owners in their neighborhoods, usually under some threat of harm if their offer was refused; and offering cash incentives to black renters to leave the neighborhood.[41]

Arguably the most effective and enduring strategy employed by these associations to achieve the goal of racial homogeneity within a neighborhood was the restrictive covenant. These covenants "were contractual agreements among property owners stating that they would not permit a black to own, occupy or lease their property." Signatories to a restrictive covenant "bound themselves and their heirs to exclude blacks from the covered area for a specified period of time [typically 20 years]. In the event of the covenant's violation, any party to the agreement could call upon the courts for enforcement and could sue the transgressor for damages."[42] The covenants were sanctioned legally by the courts, politically by local real estate boards, and "morally" by professional real estate associations. From 1924 to 1950, the National Association of Real

Estate Brokers' code of ethics stated that "a Realtor should never be instrumental in introducing into a neighborhood . . . members of any race or nationality . . . whose presence will clearly be detrimental to property values in that neighborhood. . . ."[43]

While the effects of these covenants were many, for our purposes the most important is that they denied blacks access to property that was appreciating at a relatively rapid rate, while ensuring whites' access to the same. In the Levittown, New York, housing development, for example, restrictive covenants in place until 1960 "resulted in not one Black resident among the town's 82,000 residents." Homes in Levittown that originally sold in the 1950s for a few thousand dollars appreciated to an average value of $300,000 by the year 2000. The huge appreciation in home equity in that development was thus not possible for African Americans, who were instead channeled and confined to central cities, where properties lost value.[44]

There were other legal barriers to ownership and wealth accumulation for African Americans during this period. Southern state legislatures and municipalities frequently passed "black codes" which were designed to prevent blacks from owning their own businesses by requiring them to have an employer. Beyond the statutory efforts to prevent black ownership, other extra-legal means were used to intimidate blacks from competing in the marketplace. Blacks who started businesses were often harassed, physically harmed, or even killed, especially when the new business competed with an established business of a white owner.[45]

THE STUBBORN PERSISTENCE OF ASSET DISCRIMINATION

Despite legal prohibitions against segregation and the subsequent cessation of governmental home loan practices that reinforced such segregation, private financial institutions have continued the practice of red-lining, albeit a practice that no longer limits itself to geographical location but that explicitly focuses on race. Studies have shown that even when one controls for income, blacks are still more likely to be turned down for a home loan than whites. A Federal Reserve Study published in 1991 found a "systemic pattern of institutional discrimination in the nation's banking system."[46] For example, in Boston "blacks in the highest income level faced loan rejections three times the rate of whites."[47] In 1995, Oliver and Shapiro reported that the stubborn persistence of discrimination in the housing market—practices such as redlining, racial biases in the loan approval process, and artificially inflated interest rates in loans granted to minorities—has cost "the current generation of blacks about $82 billion" and, left unchecked, will cost the next generation of African Americans $93 billion.[48]

In the wake of the banking mortgage crisis which began in 2007, a crisis that has grown increasingly worse as the months have gone by, it is clear that discriminatory banking practices continue to disproportionately harm African Americans. Indeed, 2009 may

> go down in history as the year that more African Americans fell out of the middle class than any other time in our nation's past   Best estimates are that African Americans are 2½ times are more likely to be in foreclosure than their white counterparts. At that rate, more than a million African-American homeowners will lose their home in the next four years—that's one in every five. . . . In the swirl of the sub-prime crisis, African American home ownership rates are poised to lose an entire generation of progress in a few short years. . . .[49]

The sub-prime mortgage crisis has struck African Americans especially hard because "they were specifically targeted by banks peddling dangerous sub-prime mortgages. When people applied for home mortgages, blacks were far more likely than whites to receive the high cost loans." Consistent with banking practices throughout the nation's history, these high-cost loans were not necessarily the result of the creditworthiness of the loan applicants (or lack thereof) or comparatively low incomes of African-American loan applicants. In fact, "residents in high income African-American neighborhoods are now more likely to have a sub-prime mortgage than residents in low-income white neighborhoods."[50]

As has often been the case in the past, those now suffering under the burden of high interest mortgage loans are the subject of sanctimonious moralizing by public figures.[51] Current initiatives to prevent foreclosures or restructure home loans have been challenged by those concerned about the "moral hazard" of engaging in such initiatives. There may well be moral hazards to be concerned about but it now seems clear that the hazard lies much more with those making the loans than with those receiving them. This is not to say that some of those securing loans did not act irresponsibly, but their actions are easily overshadowed by the reckless behavior of financiers pursuing unrealistic and unsustainable rates of return, actions encouraged by "regulators" and policymakers possessed of a naïve optimism in market capitalism and willful indifference to the well-documented failings of the financial industry. Every major economic collapse over the last 125 years has been preceded by the same kind of excesses in the banking industry. In each case, African Americans have paid disproportionally for the failings of this industry and for the subsequent efforts to clean up the mess left behind. In each case, financiers have used their power and access to capital to enrich themselves at the expense of those made vulnerable by their actions. In each case, the policy remedies have either ignored or failed to recognize the degree to which institutional racism has played a role in the financial difficulties of African Americans.

THE COST OF ASSET DENIAL

Needless to say, these policies and practices—from Reconstruction down to the present—have had significant effects on African Americans. The most obvious of these effects has been on the distribution of asset holdings. Dalton Conley has shown that

> in 1994, the median white family held assets worth more than seven times those of the median nonwhite family. Even when we compare white and minority at the same income level, whites enjoy a huge advantage in wealth. For instance, at the lower end of the income spectrum (less than $15,000 per year), the median African American family has no assets, while the equivalent white family holds $10,000 worth of equity. At upper income levels (greater than $75,000 per year), white families have a median net worth of $308,000, almost three times the figure of upper-income African American families ($114,600).[52]

Other more recent studies have confirmed that differences between white and black Americans with respect to wealth dwarf the income gap between the two groups. For example, Kaplan and Valls report that, in 2001, "while Black Americans earn on average 60 percent of the income of White Americans, they have, on average, only 16 percent as much wealth. This wealth gap exists at every income level, and continues even when all standard demographic variables are controlled for."[53] Kaplan and Valls argue that "a substantial portion of the wealth gap at every income level is correlated with home-ownership and the value of homes owned; much of the relative lack of wealth by Black Americans is due to the lower rates of home ownership in Black communities and the lower value of homes owned." As we have seen, lower rates of home ownership among black Americans did not arise by luck or through deliberate choices by African Americans against home purchases. Rather, the reason for the existence of the wealth gap has much to do with "the inability of Black Americans to secure credit to purchase homes on equal footing with White Americans, and the difficulty faced by everyone in securing credit to purchase homes or property in areas recognized by the lending community as predominantly Black or mixed-race neighborhoods. . . ."[54] In addition, policies and practices that effectively segregated neighborhoods by preventing black Americans from purchasing homes in white neighborhoods and discouraging or refusing to give loans to white Americans attempting to buy homes in "predominantly Black neighborhoods, artificially inflated the housing prices of homes in White neighborhoods."[55]

The combined effect of the many types of asset denial to African Americans has had a significant impact on subsequent generations and made it increasingly difficult for many black Americans to establish economic security for themselves and their families. The cumulative effects of these policies of asset denial can be seen in the following disturbing statistic: at the time of the Emancipation Proclamation, African Americans owned just 0.5 percent of the total wealth in this country. By 1990, 125 years after the ratification of the Thirteenth Amendment to the Constitution abolishing slavery, the wealth of black Americans had risen to a meager 1 percent of total wealth.[56]

If there is a silver lining in this history of asset denial, it is that the massive wealth gap in this country is due in large measure to public policy, which means it can be remedied through public policy. Those who have accumulated wealth have done so with significant institutional support put in place by public policy. Those who have not accumulated wealth have been shut out from these institutional supports *as a matter of public policy.* Thus, Oliver and Shapiro write that "the same social system that fosters the accumulation of private wealth for many whites denies it to blacks, thus forging an intimate connection between white wealth accumulation and black poverty."[57] With appropriate policies in place, this situation can be ameliorated.

CONCLUSION

The history of African Americans in the United States is not a history about which any American can be proud. The history of asset denial is but one of many kinds of exclusion and discrimination faced by African Americans. The point of recounting this history is not to claim that there is a single explanation for the magnitude of financial differences between white and black Americans today. However, it defies common sense to say that systematic efforts to prevent blacks from participating in asset-building programs to which whites had routine access are not in some way responsible for the current disparities between the wealth of whites and the wealth of blacks.

This history raises important questions about the obligations of the United States to its African-American citizens. These questions are, however, beyond the scope of this book. The purpose for recounting this history is to demonstrate that government policies can and do have a significant impact on any given citizen's ability to save and accumulate wealth. The United States continues to adopt policies that promote asset building among some, while denying it to others. Race no longer plays an *official* role in these asset-building policies; instead, this favoritism is now made largely on the basis of class. Since our asset-building policies today deliver the benefits largely by excluding certain kinds of asset-building endeavors from federal taxation, only those who pay federal taxes can take advantage of these policies. Since those who are poor do not pay federal taxes, they do not see any benefit from these policies. The question is, then, what can be done to provide similar kinds of incentives and rewards for asset accumulation to the poor.

CHAPTER FIVE

Toward Inclusive Ownership

The question is no longer whether the poor should save and build assets; instead, the question is how to help them do it.

Mark Schreiner and Michael Sherraden

The trajectory of social policy in Western democracies during the twentieth century was generally in the direction of greater political and social equality; women's suffrage, civil rights, and increases in gender equality all gesture toward a more complete inclusion of society's members. The inclusion of all persons in the benefits and rewards of *economic* life has lagged behind these developments. Today, there is reason to believe that long-term economic conditions are deteriorating for many. Recent data on income and wealth inequality continues to show a widening gap between the rich and the poor: "The top 20 percent of households earn about 56 percent of the nation's income—but command 83 percent of our wealth. The bottom 60 percent, the majority of the country, earns 23 percent of the nation's income—but owns less than 5 percent of the wealth. And the bottom 40 percent earns 10 percent of national income but owns less than 1 percent of the wealth."[1] Unless social policy begins to incorporate asset building for the poor, these inequalities will only worsen. If the trend toward inclusiveness is going to continue, those without assets will need to be given the means and mechanisms to enable them to fully participate in the life of the community.

Given the harm that comes with excluding persons from the benefits of asset-building policies, it is vital that we make asset-building policy as comprehensive as possible. An inclusive approach to asset building will require attention to all institutional mechanisms of exclusion. While exclusion on the basis of race continues to be a significant problem, it is no longer sanctioned by law. But this is not the case with respect to class. Class exclusion from the benefits of asset-building policies is a particular problem today because many of the benefits of these policies are delivered through the federal income tax code. Those who do not earn enough to pay federal income taxes are not afforded the benefits of these policies. At the same time, the value of the benefits of asset-building policies tends to be directly proportional to one's income; those with higher incomes receive disproportionately larger subsidies. As a social policy, this "Robin-Hood-in-reverse" approach makes little sense.[2] Those who are most likely to save and invest anyway hardly need larger subsidies, particularly when these subsidies drain resources that could be used to encourage and reward savings to those who most need it.

In this chapter, we will explore some practical proposals that have been put forward to distribute the benefits of asset-building policies to all persons, including the poor. These practical proposals provide a springboard for a discussion of how the norms and principles of Catholic social thought and the capabilities approach can help to shape the revision of current policies and guide the formation of future ones.

ASSET DEVELOPMENT FOR THE POOR:
RETRIEVING A LOST TRADITION

While asset-building vehicles have proliferated in recent years, the benefits have been directed largely to the middle- and upper-income levels while sharply limited for those with lower incomes. Current public policy, in other words, is acting to exacerbate wealth inequality rather than to ameliorate it, and the end result is predictable: an ever-widening wealth gap between the rich and the poor.

The use of public policy to deliver assets largely to the nonpoor marks a shift from the way in which asset-building policy has functioned for much of U.S. history. While there are obvious exceptions, U.S. wealth accumulation policies have not been limited to middle- and upper-income Americans until recently. Rather, past policies sought to expand asset ownership to those who were not yet owners. The Homestead Act, FHA guaranteed home loans, and the G.I. Bill were not policies designed primarily to help those who already had accumulated substantial wealth. Rather, these policies helped those who had little or no wealth to become owners of property and/or to develop in ways that contributed to the well-being of themselves, their families, and the nation. Re-crafting the United States' "wealth accumulation policies so that they primarily helped people with no or modest assets" would constitute a retrieval of an important tradition of American domestic policy.[3]

As has already been noted, a major reason why current asset-building policies do not include the poor is that they rely largely on the federal income tax code. Since the majority of those who are income poor do not pay federal income taxes, they are not provided with the same incentives and rewards that are built into current asset-building policies. Many of those who *have* had access to these policies and taken advantage of them have been very successful at building wealth. An important question is whether public policies designed to provide the poor with benefits in ways that are analogous to those that are now currently given to the nonpoor would be successful. Put another way, if public subsidies in the form of tax expenditures help to structure, stimulate, and materially contribute to savings for the nonpoor, is it possible that public subsidies could do the same for the poor?

For many, the question seems nonsensical. If the poor could save, would they not be doing so already? And does not poverty by definition exclude the notion of having enough left over to save? Some may even suggest that the poor are poor precisely because they have not saved and they will continue to be poor until they change their behavior. The power to make that change rests, some would argue, entirely with those who are poor. If those who are poor had made different choices, perhaps they would not be poor. The implicit (and sometimes explicit) message is this: no amount of government intervention can change the condition of those who are poor; to become nonpoor the poor must help themselves and the choice rests with them.

These questions are important, but must be accompanied by an understanding of the context within which the nonpoor and poor make efforts to save. The decisions that are made by the nonpoor occur within a particular institutional context that supports and rewards saving. This institutional context is often ignored by economists (and others). As Douglass North has said:

When economists talk about their discipline as a theory of choice and about the menu of choices being determined by opportunities and preferences, they simply have left out that it is the institutional framework which constrains people's choice sets. Institutions are in effect the filter between individuals and the capital stock and between the capital stock and the output of goods and services and the distribution of income.[4]

Recent research in the field of behavioral economics has demonstrated just how powerful the framing of decisions to save can be in determining savings behavior.[5] For example, there is a great disparity in participation rates in 401(k) plans when participants are required to opt in to the plan versus when employees are required to opt out of the plan. In one study, so-called "take up" rates in the former included about 30 percent of workers. However, when workers were automatically signed up for the plans but allowed to opt out if they so chose, take up rates shot up to 90 percent immediately and to more than 98 percent within thirty-six months.[6]

In another striking example, certain types of retirement plans in the United Kingdom are funded entirely by employer contributions. The only requirement needed to receive this benefit is for the employee to sign up for the plan. Astonishingly, barely half of the workers choose to participate in this plan.[7] Such behavior is clearly irrational and contrary to the best interest of the employee. It also demonstrates the enormous power of inertia in economic decision making. Behavioral economics seeks to take advantage of this inertia by reversing the decision-making process. By making slight alterations in how such plans are structured and administered, significant changes can be made in the participation rates of workers. Given these and other insights from the field of behavioral economics, policymakers are beginning to recognize that it is not enough to simply assume that persons will make purely rational judgments that will be to their financial benefit. Instead, it is important to develop strategies and programs that take into account real human beings and their sometimes irrational behaviors and inclinations. Building on insights from behavioral economics, Ray Boshara urges that public policy be crafted to make "savings and asset accumulation *automatic* by getting everyone into savings systems at four key occasions: at birth, at the

workplace, at tax time, and at the time when most Americans purchase their major asset, their home."[8]

Even when structures and incentives to save are present, many of
the nonpoor still find it difficult to save. It would not be surprising,
then, that those with diminished resources find it difficult to save in the
absence of institutional support and material rewards. Indeed, for the
poor, institutional factors often undermine their efforts to save. Asset
limits on income support programs, disproportionately high interest
rates on mortgage loans, and banking practices such as red-lining are
part of an institutional context that impede, discourage, prevent, and
even penalize those poor who try to save. Given this context we ought to
be surprised if anyone who is poor does manage to save.

But the question remains: would the ability of the poor to save be
enhanced if they did have access to institutions and incentives that encouraged them to save? This was the question that Michael Sherraden
began asking sometime in the late 1980s. Sherraden makes it clear that
his interest in the question of whether and how the poor could be enabled to save was not the product of an exercise in abstract problem
solving with respect to poverty. Still less did it issue from his review of
empirical research about the ability of the poor to save. Instead, the im-
petus for his focus on asset accumulation for the poor came out of conversations he had been having with those living in poverty.[9] One of the
fruits of Sherraden's questioning was a highly innovative proposal for
helping the poor to save, something he called the individual development account or IDA. Described in print for the first time in 1989,[10] the
idea became a reality in the 1990s. Sherraden's idea was a matched savings account designed specifically to enable those persons living on low
incomes to save enough for a down payment on a home, to pay for post-
secondary education, or to secure start-up capital for a small business.[11]
Sherraden's original idea has given rise to a proliferation of programs
and policies—both proposed and actual, here and abroad—aimed at
helping the poor to save and accumulate wealth.

Individual Development Accounts

Like the individual retirement account or IRA, individual development
accounts or IDAs are set up in financial institutions by the owner of the
account. Just as IRAs are subsidized by the government through tax

expenditures, IDAs are subsidized either through the government (in the form of direct expenditures) or by non-profit organizations. When an IDA account holder deposits money into the account, that money is matched according to a predetermined formula. IDAs also have restrictions on how they can be used. IDA account holders can withdraw their deposits at any time, but unless the withdrawn money is spent within some predefined category, the depositor will lose the match. So-called "matched withdrawals" are those that are spent on an asset-building endeavor, such as homeownership, college education, or owning a small business. IDA account holders are also required to attend courses in financial education on a range of issues, including personal financial planning and credit and debt management.[12]

There are today between 500 to 1,000 IDA programs[13] and as many as thirty states have included IDAs in their welfare reform plans. Thirty-four states, Washington, DC, and Puerto Rico have passed some form of IDA legislation.[14] At the federal level, "IDAs have been incorporated in the TANF program;[15] welfare-to-work funding following the 1996 welfare reform; a refugee resettlement program; the Bank Enterprise Awards program at the U.S. Treasury Department; and the Community Reinvestment Act."[16] In addition, in 1998, Congress passed the Assets for Independence Act, which provided $125 million for a five-year IDA demonstration project to evaluate the efficacy of IDA accounts.[17]

The results from the first large-scale demonstration of Individual Development Accounts, known as the American Dream Demonstration (ADD), as well as several other IDA initiatives, are encouraging.[18] The data collected thus far support the hypothesis that the poor can and do save, and that IDAs have a positive effect in stimulating saving. The results of the ADD study, which considered the IDA savings of 2,353 program participants, include the following: the average amount of time that participants held an IDA was 26 months; approximately 31 percent of ADD participants had made matched withdrawals as of 2003; among participants who succeeded in saving one hundred dollars or more, "the average net deposit was $537, the average monthly deposit was $21, and about 35 percent made matched withdrawals. The average value of matched withdrawals (including matches) was $2,711."[19]

While the magnitude of the accumulated savings is not very large, particularly when considered from the perspective of the nonpoor, one needs to keep in mind several things. First, these data represent what was saved over a limited period of time. Presumably, longer time periods would yield significantly higher savings balances. Second, the "data on matched withdrawals . . . suggest that participants do use IDAs to purchase assets expected to have high returns and that mark key steps in the life course."[20] For example, the largest portion of the matched withdrawals were used for home purchases (28 percent), to start businesses (23 percent), for post-secondary education (21 percent), and for home repair (18 percent). Finally, "participants in qualitative components of the evaluation of ADD say that their asset accumulations have changed their outlooks for the better."[21] In particular, 93 percent of IDA account holders reported they felt more confident about the future and attributed the reason for this to the fact that they now held an IDA, 84 percent reported that they felt more economically secure, and 85 percent felt more in control of their life.[22] These psychological benefits may well turn out to be one of the more significant benefits provided by IDAs. Empirical literature supports the idea that assets have positive effects that go beyond the obvious financial benefits. They have been shown to have "a positive effect on expectations and confidence about the future; influence people to make specific plans with regard to work and family; induce more prudent and protective personal behaviors; and lead to more social connectedness with relatives, neighbors, and organizations."[23]

While the data collected from the ADD study look promising, it is important to keep in mind that the significance of the proposed policy lies not with the particular mechanism for asset development it proposes (IDAs). Rather, what is significant about the IDA proposal is the *underlying change in public policy it represents*; namely, that income alone is not a sufficient mechanism for the alleviation of poverty. Within the context of recent policy initiatives aimed at reducing poverty, IDAs are arguably the embodiment of a *paradigm shift* in how poverty is understood and, in light of this understanding, how the problem of poverty should be addressed. Poverty involves deprivations in those things persons need in order to survive day to day, and for this reason income support policies remain a vital tool in ameliorating the effects of poverty. But poverty also involves deficiencies in resources needed to develop economically. Asset-building policies for the poor, including IDAs, are significant because they recognize this reality and target these resources to those who most need them. Given that the data from the ADD support the case that the poor can and do save when provided with the incentives and institutional framework within which to do so, it will be difficult in the future to defend approaches to poverty reduction that do not incorporate some means to facilitate asset accumulation. The latter may be accomplished through IDAs or through some other policy mechanism, but stubborn adherence to the idea that income support alone is a sufficient policy response to poverty would seem to be both unwise and counterproductive.

Beyond IDAs

The Individual Development Account has given rise to other promising ideas that build upon insights and knowledge garnered from research on IDAs. One of the more promising policy innovations—the Child Savings Account (CSA)—seeks to provide an asset account to every person from the moment they are born. Many economically advanced countries already have children's allowances consisting in monthly payments to families with children. The difference between a children's allowance and a CSA, however, is that the former is essentially income support while the latter is an asset initiative. Western European countries spend about 1.8 percent of GDP on children's allowances. A similar commitment to CSAs by the U.S. government would amount to $2,000 per year for *every* young person from birth to age eighteen.[24]

There are several compelling reasons for focusing asset-building accounts on children. First, such accounts can take maximum advantage of the benefits of compound interest. Because compounding effects of interest take time, the sooner such accounts are opened, the better. Second, such accounts could help to promote a culture of saving from an early age. Loke and Sherraden have argued, for example, that child-based asset-building policies may have a "multiplier effect by engaging the larger family in the asset-accumulation process."[25] Family members who have not regularly engaged in saving may come to see the benefits of it, and parents may be more likely to encourage their children to save. It is also possible that this "multiplier effect" could go beyond the family to the broader culture, providing an alternative to the consumerist culture that dominates the United States and at least some other developed countries. CSAs could form the basis for lessons in basic finance in school, something already occurring in the United Kingdom as part of their Child Trust Fund.[26] Finally, focusing on asset accounts from birth would help to mitigate to some degree the vast inequalities that currently exist from birth. Sherraden, for example, argues that "asset-based policies for children may . . . be the most direct and effective way to alter class reproduction and diminish intergenerational transmission of poverty."[27]

There are several different kinds of proposals aimed at helping children to save. In the United States, Longman and Boshara have proposed a version of a CSA—the American Stakeholder Account (ASA)— which stipulates that $500 be deposited into an account for each child at birth.[28] In addition, an ASA would automatically be created for every child under the age of eighteen to which any family member or interested party (including the account holder) could contribute. Like the IDA (and IRA), restrictions would be placed on ASAs limiting when withdrawals could be made and for what purpose they could be spent. Withdrawals could not begin until the account holder reached eighteen years of age, and the withdrawals made at this time could only be used to pursue post-secondary education and training. At age twenty-five, the account holdings could be used for education, to purchase a first home, or designated for retirement. At some point, every account holder would be required to return the original $500 for the benefit of future generations.

Current legislation in the United States Congress, the America Saving for Personal Investment, Retirement, and Education Act (ASPIRE), proposes accounts that are consistent with ASAs. The ASPIRE Act calls for the automatic creation of KIDS savings accounts for every newborn. In the United Kingdom, CSAs in the form of the Child Trust Fund (CTF) have been a reality for several years, "creating seven hundred thousand savers and stakeholders at birth every year."[29] Implemented in April 2005, the CTF was developed explicitly "to help people understand the benefits of saving and investing, encourage parents and children to develop a saving habit and engage with financial institutions, ensure that in the future all children have a financial asset at the start of adult life, and build on financial education to help people make better financial choices throughout their lives."[30] CTFs begin with the government making an initial contribution of £250, with an additional £250 contribution on the child's seventh birthday. An additional £250 is paid into the account of children from low-income families at birth and at age seven. Parents and others can contribute up to a total of £1,200 per year to a CTF account. The interest on the account is not taxed.[31] Canada, South Korea, and Singapore all currently have savings accounts for each newborn intended to promote education, with a particular focus on low-income households.

ARE ASSET-BUILDING PROPOSALS POLITICALLY VIABLE?

Works amplifying the original insight of Sherraden have given significant momentum to an asset perspective on poverty.[32] Moreover, during
a period characterized by increasingly bitter partisan bickering, the be-
ginnings of an unusual bipartisan coalition in support of asset-building
strategies is evidenced by increased legislative activity aimed at helping
the poor to accumulate assets as well as by high-profile political statements by significant party leaders. Former President Bill Clinton advocated asset-building programs in his first presidential campaign, signed
into law the Assets for Independence Act of 1998,[33] and later proposed a
much larger matched-savings program in the form of Individual Development Accounts (IDAs), which sought to enable savings and asset accumulation among low- and moderate-income Americans.

> Tens of millions of Americans live from paycheck to paycheck. As
> hard as they work, they still don't have the opportunity to save. Too
> few can make use of IRAs and 401-K plans. We should do more to
> help all working families save and accumulate wealth. That's the
> idea behind the Individual Development Accounts, the IDAs. I ask
> you to take that idea to a new level, with new Retirement Savings
> Accounts that enable every low- and moderate-income family in
> America to save for retirement, a first home, a medical emergency,
> or a college education. I propose to match their contributions, how-
> ever small, dollar for dollar, every year they save.[34]

In the 2000 and 2004 presidential elections, both the Republican
and Democratic presidential candidates proposed billion dollar IDA-
like initiatives in their platforms. Democratic candidate John Kerry, for
example, endorsed matched savings accounts—which he called "Empowerment Accounts"—for low-income Americans. Kerry proposed
that each "dollar saved in the account is matched and funds can only be
withdrawn to get additional education or worker training, start a business or buy a home. This innovative tool would help millions of American families start paving their path to economic success."[35]

In the 2008 presidential election season, Barack Obama proposed
federally matched savings accounts for those making up to $75,000 per
year. Savers "would receive a 50 percent match of the first $1,000 of sav-
ings deposits."[36] He also proposed to create workplace pensions with

automatic enrollment. Under this proposal, employers who do not currently offer a retirement plan would be required to enroll their employees in a direct deposit IRA.[37] A third Obama initiative involves federal funding for post-secondary education. The American Opportunity Tax Credit would "ensure that the first $4,000 of a college education is completely free for most Americans, and will cover two-thirds of the cost of tuition at the average public college or university and make community college tuition completely free for most students."[38]

Other government officials have also endorsed or proposed asset-building initiatives. In 2002, the Federal Reserve Chairman, Alan Greenspan, supported asset building programs for the poor.

> Sparse holdings of financial assets may, in part, be due to lack of access to savings vehicles such as individual retirement accounts and 401(k) retirement plans. Recognizing this possible link, community organizations have collaborated with their partners in government and the private sector to design innovative mechanisms for saving. One such vehicle is the individual development account, which state and federal government agencies have embraced as a means for facilitating saving for low-income households. Through tax benefits and matching funds, this instrument helps individuals earmark funds to achieve longer-term financial goals, such as purchasing a home, starting a business, or pursuing higher education or job training. Besides providing a structured account that offers a high incentive to save, individual development account programs require participation in financial training to help individuals continue on the path of economic betterment.[39]

As noted earlier, as of 2003, thirty-four states have already passed IDA laws.[40] Additional legislation is pending in the United States Congress: the Savings for Working Families Act, which aims to provide $450 million for 900,000 IDAs over a ten-year period.[41] Former Senator Rick Santorum (R-PA) and Senator Joseph Lieberman (ID-CT) re-introduced a version of the bill in the Senate in 2005,[42] and Representative Joe Pitts (R-PA) re-introduced a version of the bill in the House of Representatives in February 2007.[43]

Policy activity related to asset-building policies for the poor has not been limited to the United States. Australia, Canada, Colombia, Indonesia, Hungary, New Zealand, Peru, Singapore, South Korea, Uganda, and the United Kingdom are among the countries that either have or are currently developing programs that enable the poor to accumulate assets. In addition to government initiatives, a number of non-profit and for profit initiatives are directing their energies and resources toward helping the poor save and accumulate assets. Among the many organizations involved in this effort are the Corporation for Enterprise Development, *Demos*, the Ford Foundation, the Bill and Melinda Gates Foundation, the Grameen Bank, the New America Foundation, Pew Charitable Trusts, Save the Children, the Urban Institute, and Washington University in St. Louis's Center for Social Development.

THE PROMISE AND PERILS OF ASSET BUILDING FOR THE POOR

The paradigm of asset building for the poor offers both promise and perils. The promise of this policy approach is multifaceted and includes mechanisms that enable the poor to save and invest in themselves and their future, mechanisms that have been clearly lacking in traditional approaches to poverty alleviation. To highlight these benefits is not to say that other types of poverty programs are without merit or necessity. Income supports, greater opportunities for work, and higher wages are all central to a robust approach to poverty alleviation. While much attention has been paid throughout this book to the considerable promise offered by the asset-building approach, there are also dangers that must be considered.

Possible Perils of Asset-Building Policy

Important concerns have been raised about how the asset-building approach for the poor legitimates an individualistic, capitalist, consumer society by accepting this as the arena of play. As Sanford Schram observes, "Rather than trying to change the major orientation of the overall social welfare policy regime with its emphasis on promoting self-sufficiency and personal responsibility, asset-building policy discourse focuses on the more circumspect activity of tweaking those policies so that low-income individuals and families can more effectively participate in that regime."[44] There is a concern that asset-building policy encourages the poor to participate in an economy that is structured in a way that makes it impossible for the poor to succeed and therefore sets them up to fail. As Schram argues, "Asset-building policy discourse dooms social welfare policy to being limited to getting low-income families to try to succeed in capital markets that are systematically designed to ensure their failure."[45] Schram contends that it is the willingness of advocates of asset building to work within the current system that helps explain their appeal to "private foundations which in recent years have prided themselves on promoting innovative ideas for social reform that are simultaneously feasible because they do not challenge the hegemony of market logic for structuring social relations."[46] In short, the trouble with an asset-building approach is that it treats the symptoms of poverty, not the root cause which is a market economy designed to favor a few at the expense of the many. Asset building may help at the margins but real, long-lasting, and substantive support for those who are poor will be achieved when large, structural changes are made to the entire economic system.

A related concern is that the benefits often associated with asset-building policies—i.e., greater self-sufficiency, protection against economic shocks, increased social and political involvement—can work to reinforce the dominant cultural ethos of individualism while encouraging a purely instrumental understanding of social and political relationships.[47] Thus, for example, one reason for stressing the goal of home ownership is that it will connect the owner to a network of persons who are better positioned to facilitate access to better jobs. Understood in this way, stable relationships within a neighborhood of homeowners can come to be seen as valuable simply because they are capable of delivering ever more benefits to the homeowner. In this way, the asset-building approach may contribute to the commodification of social and political relationships and reinforce a cultural tendency to consider only "what's in this for me?"

Another troubling aspect of asset-building initiatives is that they do not address directly the daily needs of those living in poverty, which are pressing and manifold and need to be adequately attended to before less immediate needs become relevant. Jared Bernstein suggests that "[a]sset-building cannot quickly put out the flame of poverty and economic despair. That task lies with income and consumption related policies." While he does go on to note that "[o]nce the flame is extinguished, assets can help ensure it doesn't reignite," the primary task for policy should be to address the most dire needs of those living in poverty. In other words, the central focus of poverty policy ought to be on income support, a living wage, and other forms of direct subsidies.[48]

There is also considerable anxiety among some progressives that asset-building policies might erode public and political support for income-based poverty policies. To be sure, those who support asset-building policies frequently stress that such policies are intended to complement income-support initiatives, not to replace them. Still, among conservatives and others, the view persists that income-support approaches to poverty "breed dependence." This dependency has helped limit public enthusiasm for income-support policies, making them politically vulnerable. To the degree that asset-building approaches are seen as "breeding hope" rather than dependence, some worry that they "could become a Trojan horse for undermining existing welfare provision."[49]

A practical concern with asset-building policies is that the stress they place on expanding ownership may encourage those who are poor to make unwise investments and become saddled with debt they can ill afford. As noted in chapter two, the current mortgage crisis lends credibility to such concerns. Others worry that if everyone, including the poor, have a right to private ownership, the effect of asset-building policy will be to underwrite ever-increasing consumption and waste of our natural resources, increasing the burden on an already overtaxed environment. Finally, there is concern that there will not be enough political support to fund asset development for the poor at levels that will really make a difference. On this view, advocates of asset-building policies may have the best intentions but political realities will limit the support provided to the poor, limiting the 'real world' effect of such policies. At the same time, the success of asset policy initiatives may have the unintended effect of draining resources away from alternative proposals that could address the immediate needs of those who are poor.

The Promise of a Just Asset-Building Policy

In order to address these concerns, as well as to help realize the full promise of the asset-building approach, it will be useful to situate the debates about asset building within a moral framework. Sarah Moses observes that "[o]ne of the functions of our traditions of ethical thought is to provide our everyday practical decision-making with a larger moral vision within which to deliberate and act."[50] The concern is how policy development should proceed and in particular what norms and principles ought to guide it. Within Catholic social thought, the principles of human dignity, the social nature of the person, human freedom, the common good, and the preferential option for the poor contribute to a vision of social justice that is particularly salient to the development of policies aimed at alleviating poverty through asset development, and speaks to their promises and perils. Catholic social thought has consistently claimed that the norms and principles it puts forward are, or at least ought to be, relevant to evaluating and formulating public policy. While it often defers to policymakers on specific application of the norms and principles that form the basis of its teaching, the Church has frequently advocated very specific socioeconomic policies. The promotion of a living wage, the right to private property, and the recommendation that fiscal policy and monetary policies be coordinated around a goal of full employment are three such examples of particular recommendations. It is consistent with the tradition of Catholic social thought to use its basic norms and principles to provide a moral vision for a specific policy innovation—in this case, asset building—and they can also be used to enrich discussion and debate about the future direction of asset-building policy.

Martha Nussbaum's capabilities approach can also provide a moral vision to guide the formation of public policy. Nussbaum's approach begins by reflecting upon human functions—"what people are able to do and to be"[51]—and develops a list of central capabilities that promote various "doings and beings"[52] integral to the good human life. Nussbaum believes that this list of central capabilities—which she also describes as a list of "core human entitlements"—can and should be used to guide and evaluate governmental policies, including social and economic policies.[53]

Normative Contributions from Catholic Social Thought. Both Catholic social thought and the capabilities approach begin with a fundamental commitment to protecting and promoting human dignity. In Catholic social thought, human dignity is not based upon individual achievement, moral virtue, or social status, but is instead grounded in the belief that all persons are created in the image of God. This belief means that all persons have an inherent value, that they are in some sense sacred, and that therefore they are to be honored, respected, valued, protected, and cared for. It is important to stress that this is not an exclusive teaching that applies only to Catholics or to believers, but rather applies to all. It is especially important to affirm that the poor and the marginalized are children of God and reflect God's image. The dignity of the human person places claims on society, particularly when persons are marginalized and thus forced to live in conditions that undermine that dignity. Persons who lack the basic necessities in life—food, clothing, shelter—must be provided with those basic necessities. Poverty policy has attempted to address these important areas of human need, but it has been overly focused on subsidizing day-to-day necessities with almost no focus on long-term development. The Church's understanding of the protection and promotion of human dignity requires much more. It requires that persons thrive, not merely survive. The Church agrees with Bernstein and others that basic economic and social supports need to be provided, but that human dignity is not fully honored and protected simply by meeting minimal basic needs. To the degree that asset building contributes to human flourishing, the Church's teachings would support such policies. The crucial question from the perspective of Catholic social thought is whether asset-building policy can be constructed in such a way that it facilitates the flourishing of human persons, especially those who are poor. Making that judgment requires that additional norms be taken into account.

Within Catholic social thought, a crucial aspect of thriving involves full participation in society. The stress on participation as an aspect of human dignity is related to another central tenet of Catholic social teaching—the social nature of the person. Persons are created to be in community with others and it is through active participation and self-giving that they have the opportunity to actualize who they are meant to be.[54] Thus Catholic social thought can be understood to link human freedom to our inherent sociality. As Kenneth Himes observes, "The Catholic concern for a person's ability to participate in the life of a community rather than any individualistic notion of freedom abstracted from social relations offers an alternative formulation" to the more individualistic conception of the person that dominates U.S. self-identity and culture.[55] Human freedom is not primarily a freedom *from* interference or impingement, but rather it is a notion embedded in relationality, a freedom *for* participation in and contribution to community life. In other words, community and freedom are interrelated concepts within Catholic social teaching, an idea succinctly captured in the title of David

Hollenbach's essay, "A Community of Freedom."[56] Catholic social teaching, therefore, resists any conception of the relationship between individual and community that makes one an instrument of the other. In community we are encouraged to live for others, not just for ourselves.

This understanding of the interrelationship of individual and community provides an alternative discourse that can be used to counter the discourse of commodification that concerns some critics. The Catholic Church can use its considerable influence to shape the dialogue and debate about asset building in ways that help persons to understand that this approach need not be viewed as an extension of the more dominant market-based approaches to human interaction. It can draw on its deep traditions of social justice to provide an alternative and inspiring vision within which to situate asset-building policy. It would be premature at this point to specify exactly what form that vision would take in particular manifestations of asset-building policy. However, Longman and Boshara's proposal for child savings accounts takes an important step in this direction by requiring that the beneficiaries of the policy return the principle to the community.[57] In this way, the interrelationship between the individual and the community becomes embedded in the policy itself.

Current poverty policy has also tended to construe the poor as objects of charity who have little, if anything, to contribute to the larger human community. Accordingly, policies themselves are not formulated with any particular vision of the poor as active and contributing members of society. Defining the poor primarily according to their need limits the types of policies that might be envisioned as well as limiting the notion of human dignity by truncating the avenues for participation in community life. Catholic social thought can function to stimulate the public's imagination to envision a different approach to policy, one that intimately connects a profound respect for human dignity with active participation in social life.

Another important principle of Catholic social thought, the preferential option for the poor, directs attention especially to those who have been marginalized from full participation in the human community. From the perspective of Catholic social thought one of the most damaging aspects of poverty is that the poor are cut off from the benefits of society to which the nonpoor routinely have access. Public policy, therefore, should aim at including the poor in all those policies that enable human flourishing. Wherever there is a choice to be made about the use of public resources aimed at human prospering, the poor should be given priority. One of the concerns raised above focuses upon whether or not there is sufficient political support for asset-building policies in order to offer subsidies that would be substantial enough to make an actual difference in the lives of the poor. In part, this concern is based upon studies of IDA accounts in which account holders were able to save what the critics judged to be negligible amounts (e.g., around $2,500). The size of the savings was due in part to savings caps but it was also related to the limited timeframe in which savings occurred. Nevertheless, it seems clear that effective asset-building programs for the poor will require investments on an order of magnitude greater than what we have seen thus far. The preferential option for the poor would support this increase, especially when the wealthiest members of society are disproportionately favored in our current asset-building initiatives.

Those working on asset-building policy already recognize the importance of giving preference to the poor. For example, Michael Sherraden points out that "in every country in the world" asset-based policy is regressive. He suggests that one of the norms for asset-based policy ought to be progressivity, and asset accounts should be designed around "progressive deposits into the accounts of the poor." Sherraden also identifies "inclusiveness" as a norm that should guide the formulation of asset-building policy. He argues that the "goal should be an asset-based policy that is large scale and fully inclusive, with progressive funding, so that everyone participates and has resources for life investments and social protections. Everyone should have equal access to the asset-based system."[58] The preferential option for the poor can offer a useful moral warrant for Sherraden's notion of progressivity and inclusiveness.

The final principle that we will consider here is that of the common good. Like the principles of human dignity, sociality and participation, and the preferential option for the poor, the principle of the common good can also contribute to a moral vision of asset building that is truly inclusive, progressive, and participatory. The emphasis on the common good in Catholic social teaching functions as an important corrective to the excessive individualism in American culture. It is not that Catholic social thought eschews the good of individual persons; it does not. As Kenneth Himes notes, "The common good cannot be defined in abstraction from the well-being of the individuals who make up society."[59]

However, in addition, Catholic social thought sees the good of individual persons as dependent upon and integrally related to the good of the whole community. The communal nature of the common good means that it needs to be understood as "a social reality in which all persons should share through their participation in it."[60]

In recent Catholic social thought on the common good, there has been a greater emphasis on the "planetary common good," which takes into account the good of the whole creation. For those who worry that asset-building policy simply feeds into a capitalist, consumerist society with its emphasis on conspicuous consumption, there is a concomitant concern that asset-building for the poor will encourage a kind of behavior that has been contributing to the denigration of the environment and improper stewardship of the earth. Here again, Catholic social thought would provide important cautions and limits. As Pope Paul VI has said, "Increased possession is not the ultimate goal of nations or individuals. . . . The exclusive pursuit of possessions [is] an obstacle to individual fulfillment and to man's true greatness. . . . [B]oth for nations and for individual men, avarice is the most evident form of moral underdevelopment."[61] John Paul II confirms and extends Paul VI's caution in the distinction he makes between being and having. "To 'have' objects and goods does not in itself perfect the human subject, unless it contributes to the maturing and enrichment of that subject's 'being,' that is to say unless it contributes to the realization of the human vocation as such."[62] John Paul characterizes the current distribution of material goods in this way:

> [T]here are some people—the few who possess much—who do not really succeed in 'being' because, through a reversal of the hierarchy of values, they are hindered by the cult of 'having'; and there are others—the many who have little or nothing—who do not succeed in realizing their basic human vocation because they are deprived of essential goods.[63]

Thus from the perspective of Catholic social thought, asset-building policies would need to be constructed in such a way that they would avoid not only overconsumption but that they would also foster fuller development of our authentic humanity. For John Paul, of course, the fullest and most complete development of the human person has a transcendent dimension, but this does not negate the importance of material well-being or the fostering of higher human capacities, such as the development of intellect and the love and care that we are capable of offering to others. Most proposed asset-building policies place limits on what the accumulated savings can be used for, and in every case these limits exclude items that could be associated with frivolous consumption. The priority that the Catholic tradition gives to *being* over *having* and to an attitude of stewardship toward the earth can help to shape savings and asset accumulation in the direction of conservation rather than overuse and consumption.

Normative Contributions from the Capabilities Approach. Martha Nussbaum's capabilities approach can also provide a constructive moral vision to help guide the formation of asset-building policy while also helping policymakers address worries about the potentially pernicious affects of asset-building policies for the poor. Like Catholic social thought, Nussbaum begins "with a conception of the dignity of the human being"[64] and argues that there are central human capabilities "implicit in the idea of a life worthy of human dignity."[65] With the capabilities approach, attention is drawn to the common needs, capacities, and aspirations of persons that cut across cultures, traditions, and historical context. For Nussbaum, as for Catholic social thought, the fulfillment of these wants and needs and the development of these capacities depend heavily on a society that is organized to address the former and develop the latter. Here, she agrees that there are problematic structural issues in society that can impede human flourishing. Unless society is changed in ways to support the development of capacities in every person, it would not be a just society from the perspective of the capabilities approach. An asset-building policy that simply reinforced the status quo and did nothing to expand the development of capacities to all persons would be rejected by the capabilities approach. Most actual or proposed asset-building policies do aim at developing capacities in persons, in part by restricting the use of asset accounts to capability-building expenditures. In addition, since public policies have the potential to shape behavior and awareness, inclusive asset-building initiatives that reward saving and the development of central human capabilities could act as a buffer to excessive consumerism throughout a whole society. In other words, such policies have the potential to affect the *zeitgeist* of a culture, having a transformational effect, rather than maintaining or reinforcing the status quo. The capabilities approach offers a moral framework that may help to shape the development of asset-building policy in a direction that transforms existing attitudes and structures away from conspicuous consumption and toward responsible stewardship.

Nussbaum emphasizes the presence or absence of human capabilities as a measure of human well-being, an emphasis that contributes to an understanding of human freedom that has resonance with Catholic social thought. In each account, human freedom is not simply a given but arises from a complex constellation of personal and social practices that must be carefully cultivated. Persons must strive to live a life consistent with their essential capabilities and societies must recognize that the lives of their fellow citizens "have material and institutional necessary conditions."[66] Nussbaum argues that "if one cares about people's powers to choose a conception of the good, then one must care about the rest of the form of life that supports those powers, including material conditions."[67] The stress on necessary material conditions within the capabilities approach addresses a particular criticism of asset-building policies; namely, that they risk depleting resources that could be used to meet the immediate needs of the poor. Nussbaum is careful to include in her list of central human functional capabilities categories that address basic physical needs, including adequate food, shelter, and health care. She insists that we "cannot satisfy the need for one of them by giving a larger amount of another one. All are of central importance and all are distinct in quality."[68] Thus any public policy initiatives that took away from meeting these basic needs in order to support some other agenda would not be endorsed by the capabilities approach. At the same time, the moral vision provided by this approach insists that public policies go beyond the provision of basic bodily needs to include a whole range of human capabilities. Among these is control over one's environment, which for Nussbaum includes "being able to hold property . . . not just formally but in terms of real opportunity. . . ."[69] Thus the incommensurability of human capabilities helps to justify morally not just the provision of basic necessities associated with income-based poverty policy but also the necessity of facilitating ownership for all and the need for asset-based policies to help make this a reality.

Nussbaum also insists that the presence or absence of certain capacities gives persons a claim on society that those capacities be fostered in order that they be realized. She argues that the actualization of capabilities requires both the development of individual capabilities as well as external conditions to facilitate their exercise. Her emphasis on the social nature of the human person provides a way to address the concern that asset building simply encourages the poor to participate in an economy that is structured in a way that makes it impossible for them to succeed. It does this by noticing that not only are human beings dependent upon social institutions for the development of the essential functional capabilities, but they are also dependent upon these same structures for their exercise. She thus recognizes the importance of policies, laws, regulations, and practices for the development of the full range of capabilities that contribute to human well-being. This perspective on capabilities suggests asset accumulation depends not only on policies that enable the accumulation of assets but also on a range of external conditions that enable their use in ways that actually enhance human well-being. To take a relatively simple example (which is nevertheless complex with respect to the social processes involved), most asset-building policies for the poor include not only mechanisms to help the poor save but also educational programs aimed at creating financial "literacy." Financial literacy can be understood as a capability that can contribute to prudent decision making in financial matters.[70] However, the practice or exercise of financial literacy depends not only on mastering the basics of personal financial management but also upon external conditions that facilitate the exercise of those capacities. For instance, the knowledge that saving and compound interest can have important benefits over time must be matched by access to institutions that facilitate saving and reward it with interest-bearing accounts.

With respect to access to financial institutions, the poor face many obstacles, which have grown over the past several decades. For example, the deregulation of the financial services industry that began in the 1980s contributed to the flight of mainstream financial institutions from low-income neighborhoods. At the same time, the imposition of relatively high minimum balance requirements and near zero interest rates on small accounts marginalized persons of limited means. These changes contributed to a proliferation of persons with no formal relationship to a traditional bank or credit union. The growing number of the so-called "unbanked" make use of a "fringe" banking system composed primarily of insufficiently regulated pawnshops and check-cashing outlets (CCOs).

There are *no* federal regulations governing pawnshops and few states regulate CCOs, while "even fewer monitor practices in the industry or devote meaningful resources to enforcing regulation."[71] These institutions charge upward of 200–250 percent for small, secured loans, and check-cashing fees of 1.5 to 2.5 percent of the face value of the check. The resulting rapid growth in this industry is therefore not surprising—it is a very profitable industry.[72] There are, in fact, "more pawnshops today, both in absolute numbers and on a per capita basis, than at any time in United States history" and CCOs have experienced exponential growth since the deregulation of the financial services industry began in the 1980s.[73]

In this context, the exercise of practical reason in money matters is undermined by an environment that provides few options to act in ways consistent with reasoned financial judgment. Elizabeth Johnson and Margaret Sherraden have argued that "without changes in institutional access [for those currently marginalized from traditional financial institutions], financial education could even have negative effects."[74] They offer the hypothetical example of a student who attends a middle school financial literacy course that stresses the benefits of opening a savings account at an early age. Suppose that this student then "goes to a nearby bank with her $50 earnings from baby sitting . . . only to find that she must have $300 to open an account—and on top of that the teller treats her unkindly." It seems plausible, as these authors argue, that this experience "could result in an enduring negative association with banks and diminished capability to act in her best financial interests in the future."[75] Here, the absence of supportive external conditions that contribute to savings impedes the functioning of an important capability. The capabilities approach's concern for social justice combined with its robust conception of the person as social means that it cannot ignore social and institutional obstacles to the exercise of human capabilities. When economic arrangements are such that even when persons possess capabilities they cannot exercise them, the capabilities approach insists that these institutions be challenged. The capabilities approach, therefore, directs asset-building policies to attend not only to individuals but also to the structures upon which individuals depend.

Overall, the capabilities approach provides a moral perspective within which to understand the real meaning and purpose of assets, which is that they contribute to and help support human flourishing.

The way assets do this is complex. The presence of assets can have a powerful influence in developing a sense of personal agency by, for example, expanding the imaginative possibilities for one's life. As Anthony Bebbington argues, assets are "as much implicated in empowerment and change, as they are in survival and 'getting by'."[76]

Catholic social thought and the capabilities approach can provide a broad vision of social justice within which asset building for the poor can be understood and developed. The moral reasoning within these two perspectives can provide warrants for the enactment of policies aimed at helping the poor to save and accumulate assets. They can also help shape public debate and discourse about these policies. Because they draw from religious and philosophical traditions that are shared by persons from a wide range of political perspectives, they may help to identify common cares and concerns that can become the basis for meaningful and substantive discussions about the need to develop a broader approach to poverty policy. Both Catholic social thought and the capabilities approach remind all parties that important religious and moral traditions have shown and continue to show deep care and concern for those at the margins of society as well as the commitment to develop policies that encourage the participation of all.

Appendix: A Primer on
Modern Catholic Social Teaching

BEGINNINGS

'Catholic social teaching' is a term commonly applied to a body of Roman Catholic ecclesiastical writings addressed primarily to human social relations.[1] Pope Leo XIII's *Rerum Novarum* (1891) is often taken as the starting point for *modern* Catholic social teaching, although the Church had obviously been reflecting upon social and political matters long before the publication of *Rerum*. Since that encyclical, subsequent popes have usually issued one or more social encyclicals, often on the anniversary of *Rerum Novarum* and this recurrent pattern of celebrating *Rerum* is one of the reasons why it has come to be thought of as the starting point of modern Catholic social teaching.[2]

Rerum Novarum drew not only upon the long tradition of Christian thought that included scripture and influential theologians in the Church's long history (especially Thomas Aquinas), but it was also greatly influenced by social and intellectual developments much nearer in time to Leo's papacy. The influence of the latter upon Leo has led Michael Schuck to suggest that modern Catholic social thought really begins during a pre-Leonine era, one that he dates from around 1740 to the year before the beginning of Leo's papacy (1878). Many of the bold proposals for which *Rerum* is justly praised had already been the subject of vigorous debate among Catholics and non-Catholics in the years leading up to Leo's papacy. This should not be surprising. All human understanding is informed by the cultural and historical context from which it emerges, including the moral reflections of those interpreting and applying the insights of religious and philosophical traditions to their contemporary circumstances. The period before *Rerum* was a period of great social, political, and economic change and, just like others during this period, Catholics were engaged in assessing these changes as well as contributing to them. Thus, while *Rerum Novarum* is the first Catholic social encyclical, and therefore marks the official beginning of modern Catholic social thought, it should also be seen as the product of the interaction between the nearly 2,000-year-old moral tradition of Christianity and the more immediate intellectual, social, and cultural influences of the latter half of the nineteenth century.

THE LITERATURE OF CATHOLIC SOCIAL TEACHING

The literature of Catholic social teaching consists primarily of the following: papal writings, especially papal social encyclicals; relevant writings of other members of the Church hierarchy; and a wide range of literature published by Catholic moral theologians. While there is no official "canon" of papal social encyclicals, certain encyclicals would almost always be counted as making a significant contribution to this tradition. These encyclicals and their papal authors are listed in table 2.

However, *papal* encyclicals are not the only sources of Catholic social teaching issued by the Church's hierarchy. Church councils and associations of bishops (both national and regional) have also published texts that have made important contributions to the social teaching of the Church. Here again, there is no standard list of texts designated as "official" Catholic social teaching by non-papal officials but some of the more important texts are identified in table 3.

While there is, in some circles, a belief that the magisterium of the Church is limited to the Church's hierarchical ecclesial members, this is not the case. As Charles Curran points out, the "total church and all its members are involved in teaching and learning the theory and practice of the moral life. The Holy Spirit guides the church in this mission, and every individual Christian through baptism shares in the threefold office of Jesus as priest, teacher, and ruler."[3] It follows that Catholic lay persons,

Table 2. Papal Social Encyclicals with Significant Focus on Economic Issues

Year	Title	Author
1891	*Rerum Novarum* (The Condition of Labor)	Leo XIII
1931	*Quadragesimo Anno* (After Forty Years)	Pius XI
1961	*Mater et Magistra* (Christianity and Social Progress)	John XXIII
1963	*Pacem in Terris* (Peace on Earth)	John XXIII
1967	*Populorum Progressio* (On the Development of Peoples)	Paul VI
1971	*Octogesima Adveniens* (A Call To Action)	Paul VI
1981	*Laborem Exercens* (On Human Work)	John Paul II
1987	*Sollicitudo Rei Socialis* (On Social Concern)	John Paul II
1991	*Centesimus Annus* (On the 100th Anniversary)	John Paul II

including lay moral theologians,[4] also possess a teaching function in the Church and they can and do contribute to the formulation and development of Catholic social teaching.[5] The Second Vatican Council made clear that "social, political and economic problems are the special concern of the laity."[6] In addition, because of the complex nature of many of the questions with which Catholic social teaching is concerned, those working in disciplines other than theology—philosophers, economists, political scientists, sociologists, psychologists, public policy experts— are also important resources for all of those reflecting upon and developing Catholic social teaching. Thus, while it is true that the Church's moral vision is shaped by commitments that are, strictly speaking, theological in origin, it is also true that modern Catholic social thought is necessarily interdisciplinary in its approach. It cannot be otherwise, as the questions and challenges human beings face are intricately related to a range of social and human interaction that can be well understood only with the assistance of a variety of disciplines of human learning.[7]

Finally, it is not academics alone that contribute to our understanding of the causes and effects of poverty as well as the ways in which it might be reduced. Any effective poverty policy must incorporate the experience and insights of those who are poor. It is worth noting in this regard that Michael Sherraden reports that conversations with welfare

Table 3. A Sampling of Other Important Social Teaching Documents of the Church

Year	Title	Author
1919	*Bishops' Program of Social Reconstruction*	National Catholic War Council (USA)
1933	*Present Crisis*	U.S. Bishops' Conference
1940	*Statement on Social Order*	National Catholic Welfare Conference (USA)
1965	*Gaudium et Spes (Church in the Modern World)*	Second Vatican Council
1968	The Medellín Conference Documents	Latin American Episcopate
1971	*Justicia in Mundo (Justice in the World)*	World Synod of Bishops
1975	*This Land Is Home to Me*	Appalachian Bishops (USA)
1977	*Christian Requirements of a Political Order*	National Conference of Brazillian Bishops
1979	*Brothers and Sisters to Us*	National Conference of U.S. Catholic Bishops
1979	Final Document of the Third General Conference of the Latin American Episcopate, Puebla de Los Angeles, Mexico	Latin American Episcopate
1980	*The Church and the Problem of the Land*	National Conference of the Bishops of Brazil
1981	*Justice and Evangelization in Africa*	Statement of the Symposium of Episcopal Conferences of Africa and Madagascar
1983	*The Challenge of Peace*	National Conference of U.S. Catholic Bishops
1984	*What We Have Seen and Heard*	U.S. Black Catholic Bishops
1986	*Economic Justice For All*	National Conference of U.S. Catholic Bishops
1992	*The Future is Ours*	Pastoral Letter of the Catholic Bishops of Zambia
1995	*At Home in the Web of Life*	Catholic Bishops of Appalachia (USA)
1996	*The Common Good and the Catholic Church's Social Teaching*	Catholic Bishops' Conference of England and Wales
1999	*Economic Justice in South Africa*	A Pastoral Statement of the Southern African Catholic Bishops' Conference
2002	*Ethical and Gospel Imperatives for Overcoming Dire Poverty and Hunger*	National Conference of the Bishops of Brazil
2005	*The Cry of the Poor*	Zimbabwe Catholic Bishops' Conference
2005	*A Pastoral Letter of the Catholic Bishops of Kenya on International Debt*	Catholic Bishops of Kenya

recipients were "particularly influential" with respect to the development of his proposals for Individual Development Accounts (IDAs) which are aimed at helping the poor accumulate assets.[8]

THE INTENDED AUDIENCE OF CATHOLIC SOCIAL THOUGHT

To whom is Catholic social thought directed? Since Catholic social teaching is obviously grounded in the core beliefs and principles of Roman Catholicism, it is not surprising that an intended audience includes the Catholic faithful. But Catholic social thought also explicitly aims "to engage people from a variety of cultures and traditions in discourse" in the hope that, by doing so, it will contribute to "the common good of all."[9] At times, the effort to reach all people of "good will" has shaped the discourse of Catholic social teaching in the direction of an almost exclusively philosophical argument. Especially prior to Vatican II, Catholic social teaching tended to articulate its position more in philosophical terms than theological ones. This is not to say that there were no theological warrants for the moral positions taken nor that theological argument was completely lacking in the pre–Vatican II social teaching tradition. Rather, the *emphasis* of the pre–Vatican II tradition was on philosophical argument, particularly natural law argument, rather than explicitly theological argument. After Vatican II, the arguments tended to draw more evenly from both philosophical and theological warrants.

This effort to engage those within and those beyond the faith is at least potentially helpful to those struggling with the question of whether and how religious traditions can participate in modern societies that are increasingly pluralistic. With respect to Catholics and other Christians, Catholic social teaching reminds them that their faith is not a purely private concern. Rather, the moral concerns of Christianity are social and political as well; one cannot profess to be a Christian while shirking the responsibility to engage the wider world. But while engaging those outside of Christianity, Christians need not rely upon arguments grounded in exclusively Christian sources nor must they depend only upon beliefs that are unique to Christianity.

Notes

Note to the Introduction

1. See, for example, Larry M. Bartels, *Unequal Democracy: The Political Economy of the New Gilded Age* (New York and Princeton, NJ: Russell Sage Foundation and Princeton University Press, 2008); Doug Henwood, "Our Gilded Age," *The Nation* (June 30, 2008); and Scott Horton, "Bush's Gilded Age," *Harper's Magazine Online* (September 18, 2009), available online at www .harpers.org.

Notes to Chapter 1

1. Norman R. F. Maier, "Reasoning in Humans II: The Solution of a Problem and Its Appearance in Consciousness," *Journal of Comparative Psychology* 12 (1931): 182.

2. Ibid., 183.

3. Ibid., 188–89.

4. Stuart Rutherford, *The Poor and Their Money* (New York: Oxford University Press, 2000), 1.

5. Charles M. A. Clark, "Christian Morals and the Competitive System Revisited," *Journal of Economic Issues* 40, no. 2 (2006): 268.

6. Séverine Deneulin, Mathias Nebel, and Nicholas Sagovsky, "Introduction," in *Transforming Unjust Structures: The Capability Approach*, ed. Séverine Deneulin, Mathias Nebel, and Nicholas Sagovsky (Dordrecht: Springer, 2006), 1.

7. John Black, *Oxford Dictionary of Economics* (New York: Oxford University Press, 2003), 361.

8. Ibid., 362.

9. Michael Sherraden, "From Research to Policy: Lessons from Individual Development Accounts," *Journal of Consumer Affairs* 34, no. 2 (2000): 162.

10. See William O'Neill, S.J., "Poverty in the United States," in *Resources for Social and Cultural Analysis: Reading the Signs of the Times*, ed. T. Howland Sanks and John A. Coleman (New York: Paulist, 1993), 72.

11. Ladonna A. Pavetti, "Welfare Policy in Transition: Redefining the Social Contract for Poor Citizen Families with Children and for Immigrants," in *Understanding Poverty*, ed. Sheldon H. Danziger and Robert H. Haveman (New York and Cambridge, MA: Russell Sage Foundation and Harvard University Press, 2001), 230.

12. For more fully developed arguments of this perspective, see, among others, George Gilder, *Wealth and Poverty* (New York: Basic Books, 1981); Lawrence Mead, *The New Politics of Poverty* (New York: Basic Books, 1992); Lawrence Mead, ed., *The New Paternalism: Supervisory Approaches to Poverty* (Washington, DC: Brookings Institution Press, 1997); Charles Murray, *Losing Ground: American Social Policy 1950–1980* (New York: Basic Books, 1984).

13. Pavetti, "Welfare Policy in Transition," 269.

14. Ibid., 273. Pavetti reports that the former recipients of welfare "typically work more than thirty hours during the weeks they are employed."

15. Ibid., 269.

16. David T. Ellwood, *Poor Support: Poverty in the American Family* (New York: Basic Books, 1988), 18–25. Contrary to the beliefs of many conservatives, however, Ellwood contends that the welfare system had only limited effects on the family.

17. See, for example, Mary Jo Bane and David T. Ellwood, *Welfare Realities: From Rhetoric to Reform* (Cambridge, MA: Harvard University Press, 1994) and Mary E. Hobgood, "Poor Women, Work and the Catholic Bishops," in *Welfare Policy: Feminist Critiques*, ed. Elizabeth Bounds, Pamela Brubaker, and Mary E. Hobgood (Cleveland: Pilgrim Press, 1999).

18. Pavetti, "Welfare Policy in Transition," 269.

19. Gary Burtless and Timothy M. Smeeding, "The Level, Trend, and Composition of Poverty," in *Understanding Poverty*, ed. Sheldon H. Danziger and Robert H. Haveman (New York and Cambridge, MA: Russell Sage Foundation and Harvard University Press, 2001), 37.

20. Michael Sherraden, *Assets and the Poor: A New American Welfare Policy* (Armonk, NY: M. E. Sharp, 1991), 3.

21. Robert H. Haveman and Edward N. Wolff, "Who Are the Asset Poor? Levels, Trends and Composition, 1983–1999," in *Inclusion in Asset Building: Research and Policy Symposium* (St. Louis: Center for Social Development, Washington University, 2000), 2.

22. Throughout this book, I will use the phrases "asset building" or "asset development" as shorthand for the complete phrase, "asset building for the poor."

23. This criticism of the adequacy of current definitions of poverty and human well-being is shared by others. For example, Amartya Sen, a Nobel Prize–winning economist, argues that standard measures of development, e.g., Gross National Product (GNP) or personal income level, are inadequate indicators of development because they fail to assess whether the goal or purpose of development has been met. For Sen, this goal is the cultivation of "substantive freedoms—the capabilities—to choose a life one has reason to value" (Amartya Sen, *Development as Freedom* [New York: Anchor, 2000], 74). If the goal of development is to cultivate human capabilities, it follows that "poverty must be seen as the deprivation of basic capabilities rather than merely as lowness of incomes, which is the standard criterion of poverty" (ibid., 87). Cf. Martha C. Nussbaum and Jonathan Glover, *Women, Culture, and Development: A Study of Human Capabilities* (New York: Oxford, 1996). Here, and in many other places, Nussbaum provides a philosophical defense of the capabilities approach to human development that is consistent with, but not identical to, Sen's economic argument. The capabilities approach and its relationship to asset building and Catholic social thought are discussed at length in chapter three of this book.

24. The literature on assets and wealth does not adhere to a consistent definition of either assets or wealth. As these terms are used in the asset-building literature, they refer primarily, although not exclusively, to economic assets, financial or real (i.e., property, real estate, or other material holdings). In this same literature, the functional differences between assets and wealth vis-à-vis income are stressed. I discuss these functional differences in what follows. It is of course possible, and sometimes desirable, to speak of wealth and assets in non-financial terms (i.e., a particular quality of a person's character can be described as an asset) but, for the most part, this chapter will focus on these terms as indicators of one's financial condition.

25. Sherraden, "From Research to Policy," 162.

26. Melvin Oliver and Thomas Shapiro, *Black Wealth/White Wealth: A New Perspective on Racial Inequality* (New York: Routledge, 1995), 2.

27. Edward Scanlon and Deborah Page-Adams, "Effects of Asset Holding on Neighborhoods, Families, and Children: A Review of the Research," in *Building Assets: A Report on the Asset-Development and IDA Field*, ed. Ray Boshara (Washington, DC: Corporation for Enterprise Development, 2001), 25–50. For more recent reviews of the literature that corroborate the findings of Scanlon and Page-Adams, see Robert I. Lerman and Signe-Mary McKernan, "Benefits and Consequences of Holding Assets," in *Asset Building and Low-Income Families*, ed. Signe-Mary McKernan and Michael Sherraden (Washington, DC: Urban Institute Press, 2008), 195–206.

28. Sherraden, *Assets and the Poor*, 147–67.

29. Rosemary Bray, *Unafraid of the Dark: A Memoir* (New York: Random House, 1998), 13–15.

30. See chapter 2 for a discussion of the "preferential option for the poor" in the context of Catholic social teaching.

31. Congressional Budget and Impoundment Control Act of 1974, Public Law 93–344, sec. 3, 3.

32. Sherraden, *Assets and the Poor*, 55.

33. Leonard Burman, Eric Toder, and Christopher Geissler, "Discussion Paper No. 31: How Big Are Total Individual Tax Expenditures, and Who Benefits from Them?" (Washington, DC: Urban Institute, 2008), 13.

34. Ibid.

35. Robert A. Sunshine, *The Budget and Economic Outlook: Fiscal Years 2009 to 2019*, a report prepared for the Senate Committee on the Budget, 111th Congress, 1st sess., 2009, 15.

36. Burman, Toder, and Geissler, "Discussion Paper No. 31," 13.

37. Ibid.

38. Christopher Howard, *The Hidden Welfare State. Tax Expenditures and Social Policy in the United States* (Princeton, NJ: Princeton University Press, 1997), 25–27. The amount spent on Temporary Assistance for Needy Families (TANF) was $17.4 billion; food stamps $31.7 billion; Women, Infants, and Children food program (WIC), $5 billion. See Thomas L. Hungerford, *Tax Expenditures: Trends and Critiques*, Congressional Research Service (Library of Congress, 2006), 1–24.

39. Howard, *The Hidden Welfare State*, 27. Cf. Michael Sherraden, "Asset-Building Policy and Programs for the Poor," in *Assets for the Poor: The Benefits of Spreading Asset Ownership*, ed. Thomas Shapiro and Edward N. Wolff (New York: Russell Sage Foundation, 2001), 303.

40. Howard, *The Hidden Welfare State*, 30.

41. Hungerford, "Tax Expenditures: Trends and Critiques," 2.

42. Laurence S. Seidman, "Assets and the Tax Code," in *Assets for the Poor: The Benefits of Spreading Asset Ownership*, ed. Thomas Shapiro and Edward N. Wolff (New York: Russell Sage Foundation, 2001), 335.

43. Ray Boshara, "The Rationale for Assets, Asset-Building Policies, and IDAs for the Poor," in *Building Assets: A Report on the Asset-Development and IDA Field*, ed. Ray Boshara (Washington, DC: Corporation for Enterprise Development, 2001), 17.

44. Lillian Woo and David Buchholz, *Subsidies for Assets: A New Look at the Federal Budget, Federal Reserve System* (Washington, DC: Corporation for Enterprise Development, 2007), 9.

45. Ibid., 10.

46. Michael Sherraden, *Inclusion in the American Dream: Assets, Poverty, and Public Policy* (New York: Oxford University Press, 2005), 8–9.

47. Sherraden, *Assets and the Poor*, 68.

48. Hungerford, "Tax Expenditures: Trends and Critiques," 18.

49. Howard, *The Hidden Welfare State*, 28.

50. Michael Harrington, *The Other America* (New York: Macmillan, 1962), 161.

51. Howard E. Shuman, *Politics and the Budget: The Struggle between the President and Congress* (Englewood Cliffs, NJ: Prentice Hall, 1984), 105.

52. Sondra G. Beverly and Michael Sherraden, "Institutional Determinants of Savings: Implications for Low-Income Households and Public Policy," *Journal of Socio-Economics* 28, no. 4 (1999): 457–73.

53. Ibid., 466.

54. Ibid.

55. Sherraden, *Assets and the Poor*, 127

56. Ibid., 124.

Notes to Chapter 2

1. For a discussion of the difficulties of neutrality with respect to public argument and substantive policy decisions, see Michael J. Perry, "Neutral Politics," in *Love and Power* (Oxford and New York: Oxford University Press, 1993), 8–28.

2. These questions are adapted from Doug Hicks in regard to debates about inequality. See Douglas A. Hicks, *Inequality and Christian Ethics* (Cambridge: Cambridge University Press, 2000), 203.

3. For those unfamiliar with Catholic social teaching, see the appendix of this book for a brief primer describing the "nuts and bolts" of this tradition.

4. To say that the link between reducing poverty and expanding ownership to the poor has been present from the beginning is not to say that this has been the only proposal for reducing poverty in the social teaching literature or that it has received the same degree of attention throughout its history. Nor is it to say that the motivation for endorsing the expansion of ownership to the poor has always been the same. Nevertheless, the tradition has consistently put forward the argument that an effective means of reducing poverty would be to expand ownership to the poor.

5. Leo XIII, *Rerum Novarum*, in *Catholic Social Thought: The Documentary Heritage*, ed. David J. O'Brien and Thomas A. Shannon (Maryknoll, NY: Orbis, 1992), §35. All encyclicals may be found in numerous texts as well as online. The English translation may vary from source to source.

6. Ibid., §47. This translation from www.vatican.va.

7. Ibid., §4.

8. Ibid., §§34–35.

9. Ibid., §12.

10. One aspect of Leo's argument in favor of private ownership incorpo
rates what is sometimes referred to as a labor-based theory of property ownership. This theory is commonly associated with the political liberalism of John
Locke. According to Charles Curran, the influence of Locke's understanding of
private ownership on Leo's thinking can be traced to the Jesuit theologian Luigi
Taparelli d'Azeglio, an advisor to the pope. See Charles E. Curran, *Catholic
Social Teaching, 1891–Present: A Historical, Theological, and Ethical Analysis*,
ed. James F. Keenan (Washington, DC: Georgetown University Press, 2002),
177–78. Prior to the formation of political and legal institutions, Locke envisioned a state of nature in which individuals, working *as individuals*, cultivate
the land in such a way that it yields goods that are necessary for sustaining
human life. Through this work, the laborer and that which is labored upon
"mix" so that the former is now entitled to ownership of the latter. According
to Locke, this is both the origin of, and justification for, private property. As he
puts it: "The labor of his body and the work of his hands, we may say, are prop
erly his. Whatsoever then he removes out of the state that nature has provided
and left it in, he has mixed his labor with, and joined to it something that is his
own, and thereby makes it his property" (John Locke, *The Second Treatise of
Government*, ed. Thomas P. Peardon [Indianapolis: Bobbs-Merrill, 1960], 17).
One can see this Lockean view of private property reflected in *Rerum Novarum*
when, for example, Leo says "when man thus spends the industry of his mind
and the strength of his body in procuring the fruits of nature by that act he
makes his own that portion of nature's field which he cultivates—that portion
on which he leaves, as it were, the impress of his own personality, and it cannot
but be just that he should possess that portion as his own, and should have a
right to keep it without molestation" (*Rerum Novarum*, §7). Despite the fact
that there is considerable tension between Locke's understanding of political
society and that of Catholic social thought, something like a labor theory of
private ownership has persisted down to the present. See, for example, John
Paul II in *Laborem Exercens*: "From the beginning there is also linked with
work the question of ownership, for the only means that man has for causing
the resources hidden in nature to serve himself and others is his work. And to
be able through his work to make these resources bear fruit, man takes over
ownership of small parts of the various riches of nature: those beneath the
ground, those in the sea, on land or in space" (in *Catholic Social Thought: The
Documentary Heritage*, ed. David J. O'Brien and Thomas Shannon [Maryknoll,
NY: Orbis, 1981], §12).

11. Leo XIII, *Rerum Novarum*, §5.

12. Ibid.

13. "But it is precisely in this power of disposal that ownership consists,
whether the property be land or movable goods. The *socialists*, therefore, in

endeavoring to transfer the possessions of individuals to the community, strike at the interests of every wage earner, for they deprive him of the liberty of disposing of his wages, and thus of all hope and possibility of increasing his stock and of bettering his condition in life" (ibid., §4).

14. Ibid., §10.

15. Ibid., §26.

16. Ibid.

17. Ibid., §29.

18. B. Andrew Lustig, "Property and Justice in the Modern Encyclical Literature," *Harvard Theological Review* 83, no. 4 (1990): 416.

19. Leo XIII, *Rerum Novarum*, §27.

20. Ibid., §26.

21. Ibid.

22. Michael Sherraden also holds the view that ownership has both rights and responsibilities: "In the social and political arenas, property has its duties as well as its rights. The vision of asset-based welfare policy would be of welfare *citizens* instead of welfare clients. Policy would be designed not merely to provide financial support, but also to foster participation and active citizenship" (Sherraden, *Assets and the Poor*, 190).

23. David Hollenbach, S.J., *Claims in Conflict: Retrieving and Renewing the Catholic Human Rights Tradition* (New York: Paulist Press, 1979), 51.

24. Pius XI, *Quadragesimo Anno* [1931], in *Catholic Social Thought: The Documentary Heritage*, ed. David J. O'Brien and Thomas A. Shannon (Maryknoll, NY: Orbis, 1992), §45.

25. Ibid., §49.

26. Ibid.

27. Ibid., §63.

28. Ibid., §71.

29. Ibid., §63.

30. Ibid., §57.

31. Ibid., §55.

32. Ibid., §65. Such partnerships anticipate employee stock option and profit sharing plans (ESOPs).

33. Ibid., §53.

34. Ibid., §60.

35. Ibid., §88.

36. Ibid., §61. This translation from www.vatican.va.

37. John XXIII, *Mater et Magistra* [1961], in *Catholic Social Thought: The Documentary Heritage*, ed. David J. O'Brien and Thomas A. Shannon (Maryknoll, NY: Orbis Books, 1992), §59.

38. Ibid., §109.

39. Ibid., §113. This translation from www.vatican.va.

40. Ibid., §74.

41. Ibid., §112 (O'Brien and Shannon translation).

42. John XXIII, *Pacem in Terris* [1963], in *Catholic Social Thought: The Documentary Heritage*, ed. David J. O'Brien and Thomas A. Shannon (Maryknoll, NY: Orbis Books, 1992), §20.

43. John XXIII, *Mater et Magistra*, §112.

44. Ibid., §32

45. Paul VI, *Populorum Progressio* [1967], in *Catholic Social Thought: The Documentary Heritage*, ed. David J. O'Brien and Thomas A. Shannon (Maryknoll, NY: Orbis Books, 1992), §23.

46. Ibid.

47. Ibid., §26.

48. Ibid., §22.

49. Ibid., §33. Paul VI is quoting a document from the Second Vatican Council, *Gaudium et Spes*, §§63–72 here.

50. Paul VI, *Populorum Progressio*, §34

51. Mikhail Gorbachev testified that "everything that happened in Eastern Europe during these last few years would not have been possible without the presence of this Pope, without the leading role—the political role—that he was able to play on the world scene" (from an article in *La Stampa*, English version in *The Irish Times*, 4 March 1992, 9).

52. The judgment that liberation theology is more Marxist than Christian has been widely criticized. For one example, see Juan Luis Segundo, *Theology and the Church: A Response to Cardinal Ratzinger and a Warning to the Whole Church* (Minneapolis: Winston Press, 1985).

53. Daniel Finn, "Commentary on *Centesimus Annus* (on the Hundredth Anniversary of Rerum Novarum)," in *Modern Catholic Social Teaching: Commentaries and Interpretations*, ed. Kenneth R. Himes et al. (Washington, DC: Georgetown University Press, 2004), 444.

54. John Paul II, *Centesimus Annus* [1991], in *Catholic Social Thought: The Documentary Heritage*, ed. David J. O'Brien and Thomas A. Shannon (Maryknoll, NY: Orbis Books, 1992), §30.

55. John Paul II, *Sollicitudo Rei Socialis*, in *Catholic Social Thought: The Documentary Heritage*, ed. David J. O'Brien and Thomas A. Shannon (Maryknoll, NY: Orbis Books, 1987), §42.

56. David Hollenbach, S.J., "Christian Social Ethics after the Cold War," *Theological Studies* 53, no. 1 (1992): 84.

57. John Paul II, *Centesimus Annus*, §31.

58. Finn, "Commentary on *Centesimus Annus*," 446.

59. John Paul II, *Centesimus Annus*, §6.

60. Ibid., §32.

61. Ibid., §31.

62. Hollenbach, "Christian Social Ethics after the Cold War," 84.

63. John Paul II, *Centesimus Annus*, §43.

64. Ibid., §33.

65. Ibid.

66. Hollenbach, "Christian Social Ethics after the Cold War," 85.

67. John Paul II, *Centesimus Annus*, §43.

68. National Conference of Catholic Bishops, *Economic Justice for All: Pastoral Letter on Catholic Social Teaching and the U.S. Economy* (Washington, DC: United States Catholic Conference, 1986).

69. Ibid., ch. 1, §16.

70. Ibid., ch. 1, §17.

71. Ibid., ch. 3, §§183–84.

72. Ibid., ch. 2, §74.

73. Ibid., ch. 1, §16. The bishops were well aware of deteriorating macroeconomic conditions in other parts of the world and the impact of U.S. economic and political decisions on others around the globe. See ibid., ch. 3, sec. D, §§251–92, "The U.S. Economy and the Developing Nations: Complexity, Challenge, and Choices."

74. Ibid., ch. 3, §§196–97. These recommendations are consistent with those who are pushing for public policy to include asset development for the poor. "An effective policy of full employment, that is, a stable and adequately paying job for everyone who wants to work, accompanied by medical care and decent child care, would, without question, do more to reduce income poverty than any other approach. Given the very positive regard for work in the United States, a policy of full employment seems by far the most acceptable and most productive policy for combating income poverty" (Sherraden, *Assets and the Poor*, 30).

75. National Conference of Catholic Bishops, *Economic Justice for All*, ch. 3, §199.

76. Ibid., ch. 2, §103 and ch. 3, §208, respectively.

77. Ibid, ch. 3, §200, emphasis added.

78. Ibid., ch. 2, §9, emphasis added.

79. Second Vatican Council, *Gaudium et Spes* [1965], in *Catholic Social Thought: The Documentary Heritage*, ed. David J. O'Brien and Thomas A. Shannon (Maryknoll, NY: Orbis Books, 1992), §63.

80. National Conference of Catholic Bishops, *Economic Justice for All*, "Principal Themes of the Pastoral Letter," §13.

81. Ibid., ch. 2, §40.

82. Second Vatican Council, *Gaudium et Spes*, §63.

83. O'Neill, "Poverty in the United States," 75.

84. Second Vatican Council, *Gaudium et Spes*, §26.

85. John XXIII, *Mater et Magistra*, §13.

86. Second Vatican Council, *Gaudium et Spes*, §32.

87. National Conference of Catholic Bishops, *Economic Justice for All*, ch. 2, §36.

88. Ibid., ch. 2, §77.

89. Ibid., ch. 2, §64.

90. Aristotle, *Politics*, in *Introduction to Aristotle*, ed. Richard McKeon (Chicago: University of Chicago Press, 1973), 1253a18.

91. Thomas Aquinas, "Book One: Commentary on the Nicomachean Ethics," in *Thomas Aquinas: Selected Political Writings*, ed. A. P. D'Entreves (Oxford: Basil Blackwell, 1948), 191.

92. National Conference of Catholic Bishops, *Economic Justice for All*, ch. 2, §65.

93. Second Vatican Council, *Gaudium et Spes*, §25.

94. John XXIII, *Mater et Magistra*, §65.

95. David Hollenbach, S.J., *The Common Good and Christian Ethics*, ed. Robin Gill (Cambridge: Cambridge University Press, 2002), 81.

96. Latin American Episcopate, "Puebla Final Document," in *Puebla and Beyond: Documentation and Commentary*, ed. John Eagleson and Philip Scharper (Maryknoll, NY: Orbis Books, 1979), §§29–30.

97. Pius XII, "The Internal Orders of States and People," Christmas Broadcast Message (1942).

98. John XXIII, *Mater et Magistra*, §112.

99. Second Vatican Council, *Gaudium et Spes*, §71. This translation from www.vatican.va.

100. National Conference of Catholic Bishops, *Economic Justice for All*, ch. 2, §91.

101. National Catholic War Council, "Program for Social Reconstruction in the Marketplace," in *American Catholic Social Teaching*, ed. Thomas J. Massaro and Thomas A. Shannon (Collegeville, MN: Michael Glazier Books, 1919), 51, §6.

102. National Conference of Catholic Bishops, *Economic Justice for All*, ch. 4, §300.

103. John Eagleson and Philip Scharper, *Puebla and Beyond: Documentation and Commentary* (Maryknoll, NY: Orbis Books, 1979), 264–67.

104. John Paul II, *Sollicitudo Rei Socialis*, §42.

105. Ibid.

106. National Conference of Catholic Bishops, *Economic Justice for All*, ch. 1, §24.

107. Ibid., ch. 3, §200.

108. Stephen J. Pope, "Proper and Improper Partiality and the Preferential Option for the Poor," *Theological Studies* 54, no. 2 (1993): 252.

109. Ibid., 265.

110. Carter Lindberg, *Beyond Charity: Reformation Initiatives for the Poor* (Minneapolis: Fortress Press, 1993), 22.

111. Ibid., 27–29.

112. An obvious example in this context would be Simon and Novak's *Liberty and Justice for All*, a document published by lay Catholics that was very critical of *Economic Justice for All*. See William E. Simon and Michael Novak, *Liberty and Justice for All: Report on the Final Draft (June 1986) of the U.S. Catholic Bishops' Pastoral Letter "Economic Justice for All"* (Notre Dame, IN: Brownson Institute, 1986).

113. See David F. Kelsey, *The Uses of Scripture in Recent Theology* (Minneapolis: Fortress Press, 1975), 122–212, and Lisa Sowle Cahill, *Between the Sexes: Foundations for a Christian Ethics of Sexuality* (Minneapolis: Fortress Press, 1985), 14–44.

114. See Cahill, *Between the Sexes*; Kent Greenawalt, *Private Consciences and Public Reasons* (Oxford: Oxford University Press, 1995); Amy Gutmann and Dennis Thompson, *Democracy and Disagreement* (Cambridge, MA: Belknap Press, 1996); Michael J. Perry, *Under God? Religious Faith and Liberal Democracy* (Cambridge: Cambridge University Press, 2003); and John Rawls, *Political Liberalism* (New York: Columbia University Press, 1993; reprint, 1996).

Notes to Chapter 3

1. Robert S. Boynton, "Who Needs Philosophy?" *New York Times*, November 21, 1999. The capabilities approach is also associated with Amartya Sen. Sen discusses and defends the capabilities approach primarily within the discipline of economics, while Nussbaum's approach is primarily philosophical. Sen's work, while clearly motivated by concerns about social justice, is aimed at providing a method for comparative measurement of "quality of life." See especially Sen, *Development as Freedom*.

2. Martha C. Nussbaum, *Frontiers of Justice* (Cambridge, MA: Belknap Press of Harvard University, 2007), 70.

3. Ibid., 161.

4.. Martha C. Nussbaum, "Poverty and Human Functioning: Capabilities as Fundamental Entitlements," in *Poverty and Inequality*, ed. David B. Grusky and Ravi Kanbur (Stanford, CA: Stanford University Press, 2006), 48.

5. Rawls, *Political Liberalism*, 4 and many other places.

6. Sherraden, *Inclusion in the American Dream*, 4. Sherraden makes connections between the capabilities approach and asset building for the poor in several other places. See, for example, Michael Sherraden, *IDAs and Asset-Building Policy: Lessons and Directions* (St. Louis: Washington University, 2008), 2: "Income, as a proxy for consumption, has been the standard defini-

tion of poverty in social policy. Income support is essential to provide basic necessities. But today there is increasing questioning of income as [the] sole definition of poverty and well-being. Amartya Sen . . . and others are also looking toward capabilities. Asset-based policy can be seen as part of this larger discussion, one measure of long-term capabilities. As public policy, asset building may be understood as a form of 'social investment.' . . . From this perspective, asset-based policy is a complement to income-based policy, each serving different purposes—income may support consumption or 'getting by', while assets may promote development or 'getting ahead'."

7. For an insightful discussion of this phenomenon, see Uma Naraya, "Contesting Cultures: 'Westernization,' Respect for Cultures, and Third World Feminists," in *Dislocating Cultures: Identities, Traditions, and Third World Feminism* (New York: Routledge, 1997).

8. See Jean-Francois Lyotard, *The Postmodern Condition: A Report on Knowledge* (Manchester: Manchester University Press, 1984).

9. Jack A. Bonsor, "History, Dogma, and Nature: Reflections on Postmodernism and Theology," *Theological Studies* 55 (1994): 309.

10. Martha C. Nussbaum, "Social Justice and Universalism: In Defense of an Aristotelian Account of Human Functioning," *Modern Philology* 90, Supplement (1993): S62.

11. Martha C. Nussbaum, "Human Capabilities, Female Human Beings," in *Women, Culture, and Development: A Study of Human Capabilities (a Study Prepared for the World Institute for Development Economics Research (Wider) of the United Nations University Wider Studies in Development Economics)*, ed. Martha C. Nussbaum and Jonathan Glover (Oxford and New York: Clarendon Press and Oxford University Press, 1995), 68.

12. Richard Rorty, "The Priority of Democracy to Philosophy," in *Prospects for a Common Morality*, ed. Gene Outka and John P. Reeder (Princeton, NJ: Princeton University Press, 1992), 255.

13. Nussbaum, "Human Capabilities, Female Human Beings," 68–69. One might argue that religious belief and the human experience of God is exactly the sort of thing we can affirm because it is something that, if not universal, is a widely shared human experience.

14. Martha C. Nussbaum, "Non-Relative Virtues: An Aristotelian Approach," in *Ethical Theory: Character and Virtue*, ed. Peter A. French, Theodore Uebling Jr., and Howard K. Wettstein (Notre Dame, IN: University of Notre Dame Press, 1988), 37. Cf. Aristotle, *Politics* I.2, 1253a1–18, "But he who is unable to live in society, or who has no need because he is sufficient for himself, must be either a beast or a god: he is no part of the state" (*The Complete Works of Aristotle: The Revised Oxford Translation*, vol. 2, ed. Jonathan Barnes [Princeton, NJ: Princeton University Press, 1984]).

15. Nussbaum, "Social Justice and Universalism," S54.

16. Martha C. Nussbaum, "Non-Relative Virtues: An Aristotelian Approach," in *The Quality of Life*, ed. Martha C. Nussbaum and Amartya Sen (Oxford: Clarendon Press, 1993), 261.

17. Martha C. Nussbaum, "Aristotelian Social Democracy," in *Liberalism and the Good*, ed. R. Bruce Douglass, Gerald M. Mara, and Henry S. Richardson (New York and London: Routledge, 1990), 217.

18. Ibid.

19. Ibid., 235.

20. Martha C. Nussbaum, "The Good as Discipline, the Good as Freedom," in *Ethics of Consumption: The Good Life, Justice, and Global Stewardship*, ed. David A. Crocker and Toby Linden (Lanham, MD: Rowman & Littlefield, 1998), 318.

21. Nussbaum, "Non-Relative Virtues," 38.

22. John Rawls, "The Idea of an Overlapping Consensus," *Oxford Journal for Legal Studies* 7, no. 1 (Spring 1987): 1–25.

23. Nussbaum, "The Good as Discipline," 318.

24. Nussbaum, "Human Capabilities, Female Human Beings," 72.

25. Ibid.

26. Ibid., 80. See also Nussbaum, "Poverty and Human Functioning," 52–57.

27. Martha C. Nussbaum, "Religion and Women's Human Rights," in *Religion and Contemporary Liberalism*, ed. Paul J. Weithman (Notre Dame, IN: University of Notre Dame Press, 1997), 101.

28. For Nussbaum's discussion of the link between her own thought and that of Jacques Maritain, see Martha C. Nussbaum, "Aristotle, Politics, and Human Capabilities: A Response to Antony, Arneson, Charlesworth, and Mulgan," *Ethics* 111 (2000): 105. Maritain helped draft the United Nations' *Universal Declaration of Human Rights*.

29. Nussbaum, "Human Capabilities, Female Human Beings," 80.

30. Nussbaum, "Aristotelian Social Democracy," 219. The essential capabilities of human beings that are listed in this table as well as the quoted text come from Nussbaum, *Women and Human Development: The Capabilities Approach* (New York: Cambridge University Press, 2000), 78–80. For an earlier, slightly different, version of Nussbaum's categorization of the essential limits and capabilities of human beings see Nussbaum, "Human Capabilities, Female Human Beings," 83–85, and Nussbaum, "Social Justice and Universalism," S55–S59.

31. Nussbaum, *Women and Human Development*, 78.

32. Martha C. Nussbaum, "Human Functioning and Social Justice: In Defense of Aristotelian Essentialism," *Political Theory* 20, no. 2 (1992): 222.

33. Ibid.

34. Nussbaum, *Women and Human Development*, 82.

35. Ibid., 87.

36. John Rawls, *A Theory of Justice,* rev. ed. (Oxford: Oxford University Press, 1999).

37. Nussbaum, "Human Functioning and Social Justice," 233.

38. Ibid.

39. Nussbaum, *Women and Human Development,* 60.

40. Ibid., 61.

41. Ibid.

42. Martha C. Nussbaum, "Public Philosophy and International Feminism," *Ethics* 108 (1998): 785ff. To my knowledge, this was the first time that Nussbaum discussed the importance of property rights.

43. Ibid., 789.

44. Nussbaum, *Women and Human Development,* 106.

45. Ibid.

46. Sherraden, "From Research to Policy," 176–77.

47. Sherraden, *Assets and the Poor,* 149.

48. Ibid. See also Rand D. Conger et al., "Linking Economic Hardship to Marital Quality and Instability," *Journal of Marriage and the Family* 52 (1990); G. Levinger and O. Moles, *Divorce and Separation: Contexts, Causes, and Consequences* (New York: Basic Books, 1979); and Richard J. Galligan and Stephen J. Bahr, "Economic Well-Being and Marital Stability: Implications for Income Maintenance Programs," *Journal of Marriage and the Family* 40, no. 2 (1978).

49. Sen, *Development as Freedom,* 292–93.

50. Sherraden, *Assets and the Poor,* 156.

51. Ibid.

52. Ibid., 158, citing Adam Smith, *An Inquiry into the Nature and Causes of the Wealth of Nations,* ed. C. J. Bullock (New York: P. F. Collier & Son, 1909), 222.

53. Sherraden, *Assets and the Poor,* 158.

54. Mark Schreiner and Michael Sherraden, *Can the Poor Save? Saving & Asset Building in Individual Development Accounts* (New Brunswick and London: Transaction, 2007), 23.

55. For an extended discussion of this topic, see Sherraden, *Assets and the Poor,* 125–26 and 62–64.

56. Ibid., 165–66.

57. Organization for Economic Cooperation and Development, *Asset Building and the Escape from Poverty: A New Welfare Policy Debate* (Paris: OECD, 2003), 13.

58. Michael Lind, "The Small Holder Society," *Harvard Law & Policy Review* 1 (2007): 144–47.

59. Cited in ibid., 144.

60. Ibid., 145.

61. Ibid.

62. Scanlon and Page-Adams, "Effects of Asset Holding on Neighbor-hoods, Families, and Children," 45.

63. See Oliver and Shapiro, *Black Wealth/White Wealth*, especially chapter 5, "A Story of Two Nations: Race and Wealth," 91–126.

64. The history of asset denial is discussed in detail in chapter 4.

65. Nussbaum, *Women and Human Development*, 79.

66. Sherraden, *Assets and the Poor*, 155–56.

67. Ibid., 151–52.

68. Schreiner and Sherraden, *Can the Poor Save?* 24.

69. Michael Sherraden, "From a Social Welfare State to a Social Investment State," *Shelterforce Online*, no. 128 (2003).

Notes to Chapter 4

1. Barack Obama, "'A More Perfect Union'," *New York Times*, March 18, 2008.

2. See, for example, Oliver and Shapiro, *Black Wealth/White Wealth* and Thomas Shapiro, *The Hidden Cost of Being African American: How Wealth Perpetuates Inequality* (New York: Oxford University Press, 2004).

3. Trina Williams Shanks, "The Homestead Act: A Major Asset-Building Policy in American History," in *Inclusion in the American Dream: Assets, Poverty, and Public Policy*, ed. Michael Sherraden (New York: Oxford University Press, 2005), 29.

4. Ibid., 20.

5. Ibid., 23.

6. Ibid.

7. Ibid., 20. During that same year, Congress passed another significant piece of legislation which has important implications for asset building, the Morrill Act of 1862 (also known as the Land Grant College Act, 7 U.S.C. §301 et seq.). The Morrill Act, named after Congressman Justin Smith Morrill of Vermont, offered to states land grants equal to 30,000 acres of public land for each senator and representative, which they could then sell for the purpose of financing the creation of what have come to be known as "land grant colleges." The sale of the land enabled states not only to build the colleges but also to establish an endowment to fund the operations of the college down to the present. However, in the early years of these schools, blacks were not allowed to attend southern land grant colleges (all of which were created after the Civil War). This situation was at least partially rectified by the Second Morrill Act of 1890 (also known as the Agricultural College Act of 1890, 26 Stat. 417, 7 U.S.C. §321 et seq.) which provided that "no money shall be paid out under this act to

any State or Territory for the support and maintenance of a college where a distinction of race or color is made in the admission of students" while also allowing for "the establishment and maintenance of such colleges separately for white and colored students shall be held to be a compliance with the provisions of this act if the funds received in such State or Territory be equitably divided. . . ." Among the land grant colleges are: Auburn University, Colorado State University, Cornell University, Iowa State University, Kansas State University, Louisiana State University, Michigan State University, Montana State University, North Carolina State University, North Dakota State University, Oklahoma State University, Ohio State University, Oregon State University, Pennsylvania State University, Purdue University, Rutgers University, South Dakota State University, Texas A&M University, University of Alaska, University of Arkansas, University of Arizona, University of California at Berkeley, University of Connecticut, University of Delaware, University of Florida, University of Georgia, University of Hawaii, University of Illinois, University of Kentucky, University of Maryland–College Park, University of Massachusetts–Amherst, University of Maine, University of Minnesota, University of Missouri Columbia, University of Nebraska, University of Nevada, University of New Hampshire, University of Rhode Island, University of Tennessee, University of Vermont, University of Wyoming, Utah State University, and Virginia State University.

8. Williams Shanks, "The Homestead Act," 23–24.

9. Oliver and Shapiro, *Black Wealth/White Wealth*, 13.

10. See the government archives at www.archives.gov for the complete text.

11. Claude F. Oubre, *Forty Acres and a Mule: The Freedmen's Bureau and Black Land Ownership* (Baton Rouge: Louisiana State University Press, 1978), 31.

12. Ibid., 53. Original capitalization restored.

13. Ibid., 53–54.

14. Ibid., 54.

15. Ibid., 183.

16. Ibid., 20 n.48.

17. Ibid., 19.

18. Ibid., 183.

19. Williams Shanks, "The Homestead Act," 35.

20. Ibid.

21. Oliver and Shapiro, *Black Wealth/White Wealth*, 14.

22. Oubre, *Forty Acres and a Mule*, xiii.

23. Dalton Conley, *Being Black, Living in the Red: Race, Wealth, and Social Policy in America* (Berkeley: University of California Press, 1999), 34.

24. Oubre, *Forty Acres and a Mule*, 159.

25. Ibid., 161; $31 million is equal to approximately $5.4 billion in 2007 dollars. For comparison, consider that in 1985 there were 14,000 community banks with inflation adjusted assets of just under $1 billion. See Phillip Longman and Ray Boshara, *The Next Progressive Era: A Blueprint for Broad Prosperity* (Sausalito, CA: PoliPoint Press, 2009), 73.

26. Sherraden, *Assets and the Poor*, 133.

27. Ibid., 134, citing W. E. B. Du Bois, *The Souls of Black Folk* (Greenwich, CT: Fawcett Publications, 1970), 39.

28. Conley, *Being Black, Living in the Red*, 35.

29. Trina R. Williams, *Asset-Building Policy as a Response to Wealth Inequality: Drawing Implications from the Homestead Act* (St. Louis: Center for Social Development, Washington University, 2003), 5.

30. W. E. B. Du Bois, "A Negro Nation within a Nation," *Current History* 42 (1935): 265.

31. Oliver and Shapiro, *Black Wealth/White Wealth*, 38.

32. Ibid.

33. Ibid.

34. Ibid., 17.

35. Ibid. These maps "subsequently were used by Federal Housing Authority (FHA) loan officers who made loans on the basis of these designations."

36. Ibid.

37. Douglas S. Massey, "Race, Class, and Markets: Social Policy in the 21st Century," in *Poverty and Inequality*, ed. David B. Grusky and Ravi Kanbur (Stanford, CA: Stanford University Press, 2006), 121.

38. Federal Housing Authority, *Underwriting Manual: Underwriting and Valuation Procedure under Title II of the National Housing Act with Revisions to April 1, 1936*, Part II (Washington, DC: FHA, 1936), §233.

39. Ibid., §284.

40. Boshara, "The Rationale for Assets, Asset-Building Policies, and IDAs for the Poor," 19.

41. Douglas S. Massey and Nancy A. Denton, *American Apartheid: Segregation and the Making of the Underclass* (Cambridge, MA: Harvard University Press, 1993), 36.

42. Ibid.

43. Cited in ibid., 37.

44. Boshara, "The Rationale for Assets, Asset-Building Policies, and IDAs for the Poor," 19.

45. Conley, *Being Black, Living in the Red*, 35.

46. Oliver and Shapiro, *Black Wealth/White Wealth*, 19.

47. Ibid., 20.

48. Ibid., 151.

49. Amelia Warren Tyagi, "*Marketplace* Commentary on Sub-Prime Mortgage Crisis," in *Marketplace*, ed. Kai Ryssdal (American Public Media, 2009).

50. Ibid.

51. See, for example, George Will, "Folly and the Fed," *Washington Post*, August 16, 2007. "In 2008, as voters assess their well-being, several million households with adjustable-rate home mortgages will have their housing costs increase. Defaults, too, will increase. That will be a perverse incentive for the political class to be compassionate toward themselves in the name of compassion toward borrowers, with money to bail out borrowers. If elected politicians controlled the Federal Reserve, they would lower interest rates. Fortunately, we have insulated the Federal Reserve from democracy."

52. Conley, *Being Black, Living in the Red*, 1.

53. Jonathan Kaplan and Andrew Valls, "Housing Discrimination as a Basis for Black Reparations," *Public Affairs Quarterly* 21, no. 3 (2007): 258.

54. Ibid.

55. Ibid., 259. See also David Rusk, "Social Change Strategies for the Future of Metropolitan Areas," in *Living the Catholic Social Tradition: Introduction and Overview*, ed. Kathleen Maas Weigert and Alexia K Kelley (Lanham, MD: Rowman & Littlefield, 2005), and Shapiro, *The Hidden Cost of Being African American*.

56. Conley, *Being Black, Living in the Red*, 25.

57. Oliver and Shapiro, *Black Wealth/White Wealth*, 5.

Notes to Chapter 5

1. Ray Boshara, "Poverty Is More Than a Matter of Income," *New York Times*, September 29, 2002. These inequality figures have changed marginally since the publication of this piece. More recent sources note incremental changes in inequality since 2002, but the gap between income and wealth remains substantially the same. See, for example, Lawrence Mishel, Jared Bernstein, and Heidi Shierholz, *The State of Working America, 2008/2009* (Ithaca, NY: Cornell University Press, 2009).

2. Longman and Boshara, *The Next Progressive Era*, 83.

3. Ibid.

4. Douglass North, *Structure and Change in Economic History* (New York: W. W. Norton, 1981), 201.

5. For an influential discussion of how different ways of framing alternatives impact the decision making of persons, see Daniel Kahneman and Amos Tversky, "Prospect Theory: An Analysis of Decision under Risk," *Econometrica* 47, no. 2 (1979), and Amos Tversky and Daniel Kahneman, "The Framing of Decision and the Psychology of Choice," *Science* 211, no. 4481 (1981). In 2002,

Kahneman was awarded the Nobel Prize in Economics for his work in behavioral economics.

6. Longman and Boshara, *The Next Progressive Era*, 88.

7. Richard H. Thaler and Cass R. Sunstein, *Nudge: Improving Decisions about Health, Wealth, and Happiness* (New Haven, CT and London: Yale University Press, 2008), 108.

8. See Ray Boshara, "Combating Poverty by Building Assets: Lessons from Around the World," *Pathways* (Spring 2009): 22, emphasis added.

9. See Sherraden, *Assets and the Poor.*

10. Michael Sherraden, "Individual Development Accounts," *The Entrepreneurial Economy Review* 8, no. 5 (1989).

11. Sherraden further developed the idea for IDAs in his *Assets and the Poor.* Since then, he and others have continued to refine the idea.

12. Schreiner and Sherraden, *Can the Poor Save?* 1.

13. Corporation for Enterprise Development, "Assets Newsletter" (Washington, DC, 2005).

14. Center for Social Development, Washington University at St. Louis asset-building website.

15. TANF (Temporary Assistance for Needy Families) participants could participate in IDA programs and the amount saved in the IDA was exempt from all federal means-tested programs. States could match the savings of IDA participants using TANF funds. Thus, TANF became "the first federal antipoverty policy in which asset building was no longer discouraged and, in fact, could be supported through federal funds" (Sherraden, "Asset-Building Policy and Programs for the Poor," 307).

16. Tommy Draut, David Callahan, and Corinna Hawkes, *Crossing Divides: New Common Ground on Poverty and Economic Security* (New York: Demos, 2002), 25–26.

17. Corporation for Enterprise Development, "Assets Newsletter."

18. See Mark Schreiner, Margaret Clancy, and Michael Sherraden, *Final Report: Saving Performance in the American Dream Demonstration: A National Demonstration of Individual Development Accounts* (St. Louis: Center for Social Development, Washington University, 2002); Jan L. Losby and Jill R. Robinson, *Michigan IDA Partnership: Year Three Program Evaluation Report* (Washington, DC: ISED Solutions, 2004); Mark Schreiner et al., "Assets and the Poor: Evidence from Individual Development Accounts," in *Inclusion in the American Dream: Assets, Poverty, and Public Policy*, ed. Michael Sherraden (New York and Oxford: Oxford University Press, 2005); and Schreiner and Sherraden, *Can the Poor Save?*

19. Yunju Nam, Caroline Ratcliffe, and Signe-Mary McKernan, "Effects of Asset Tests and IDA Programs," in *Asset Building and Low-Income Families*, ed. Signe-Mary McKernan and Michael Sherraden (Washington, DC: Urban Institute Press, 2008), 166.

20. Schreiner, Clancy, and Sherraden, *Final Report: Saving Performance in the American Dream Demonstration*, 49.

21. Ibid.

22. Amanda Moore et al., *Saving, IDA Programs, and Effects of IDAs: A Survey of Participants* (St. Louis: Center of Social Development, Washington University, 2001).

23. Lerman and McKernan, "Benefits and Consequences of Holding Assets," 198.

24. See Sherraden, "From Research to Policy," 168–70.

25. Vernon Loke and Michael Sherraden, "Building Assets from Birth: A Global Comparison of Child Development Account Policies," *International Journal of Social Welfare* 18 (2009): 119.

26. Longman and Boshara, *The Next Progressive Era*, 85.

27. Loke and Sherraden, "Building Assets from Birth," 119. Cf., Michael Sherraden, "From a Social Welfare State to a Social Investment State," in *Asset-Based Welfare and Poverty. Exploring the Case For and Against Asset-Based Welfare Policies*, ed. C. Kober and W. Paxton (London: Institute for Public Policy Research and End Child Poverty, 2002). Interestingly, the idea behind child savings accounts would appear to be consistent with John Rawls's articulation of what he called a "property owning democracy." Whereas a welfare state redistributes income *after* "those who need assistance can be identified," a property-owning democracy insists that the basic institutions of society "must from the outset put in the hands of citizens generally and not only a few, the productive means to be fully cooperating members of society" (John Rawls, "Preface for the French Edition of *A Theory of Justice* [1987]" in *John Rawls: Collected Papers*, ed. Samuel Freeman [Cambridge, MA: Harvard University Press, 1999], 419–20).

28. Longman and Boshara, *The Next Progressive Era*, 83–87.

29. Ibid., 84.

30. Loke and Sherraden, "Building Assets from Birth," 121.

31. Ibid.

32. See, e.g., Oliver and Shapiro, *Black Wealth/White Wealth*; Conley, *Being Black*; Thomas M. Shapiro and Edward N. Wolff, *Assets for the Poor: The Benefits of Spreading Asset Ownership* (New York: Russell Sage Foundation, 2001); and Sherraden, *Inclusion in the American Dream*.

33. See Assets for Independence Act, 42 U.S.C. §604 (1998). The legislation authorized $250 million for matched savings accounts in 1999–2009.

34. See William Jefferson Clinton, "President of the United States of America, State of the Union Address, January 27, 2000," available at usgovinfo.about.com as State of the Union Address: 1/27/2000.

35. Senator John F. Kerry, "Speech at the City Club of Cleveland, December 3, 2002," available at www.dlc.org (the Democratic Leadership Council website).

36. Reid Cramer, Alejandra Lopez-Fernandini, and Mark Huelsman, *Presidential Promises: A Review of Campaign Proposals to Promote Savings and Asset Building* (Washington, DC: New America Foundation, 2008), 4.

37. Ibid.

38. Ibid., 5.

39. Alan Greenspan, "Remarks" at the Ninth Economic Development Summit, "Economic Development and Financial Literacy," The Greenling Institute, Oakland, CA, January 10, 2002, available at www.federalreserve.gov (the Federal Reserve website).

40. See Karen Edwards and Lisa Marie Mason, "State Policy Trends for Individual Development Accounts in the United States," *Social Development Issues* 25 (2003).

41. See Savings for Working Families Act of 2007, H.R. 892, 110th Cong. § 450(h)(1)(B) (2007).

42. See Savings for Working Families Act of 2005, S. 922, 109th Cong. (2005).

43. See Edwards and Mason, "State Policy Trends for Individual Development Accounts."

44. Sanford F. Schram, *Welfare Discipline: Discourse, Governance, and Globalization* (Philadelphia: Temple University Press, 2006), 108.

45. Ibid., 110.

46. Ibid., 120.

47. Ibid., 111–16.

48. Jared Bernstein, "Work, Wages and Income Still Matter: Why Asset-Building Isn't Enough," *Shelterforce Online*, no. 128 (2003).

49. Martin Barnes, "Reaching the Socially Excluded?" in *Asset-Based Welfare and Poverty: Exploring the Case For and Against Asset-Based Welfare Policies*, ed. Claire Kober and Will Paxton (London: Institute for Public Policy Research and End Child Poverty, 2002), 14.

50. Sarah Moses, "A Just Society for the Elderly: The Importance of Justice as Participation," *Notre Dame Journal of Law, Ethics, and Public Policy* 21 (2007): 335.

51. Nussbaum, *Women and Human Development*, 5.

52. Nussbaum, "Social Justice and Universalism," 3.

53. Nussbaum, *Frontiers of Justice*, 70.

54. "The point of departure in Catholic ethics is the dignity of the human creature made to exist in God's 'image' and, from the beginning, in social interrelationship" (Lisa Sowle Cahill, "The Catholic Tradition: Religion, Morality, and the Common Good," *Journal of Law and Religion* 5, no. 1 [1987]: 75).

55. Kenneth R. Himes, "Rights of Entitlement: A Roman Catholic Perspective," *Notre Dame Journal of Law, Ethics, and Public Policy* 11 (1997): 521.

56. David Hollenbach, S.J., "Afterword: A Community of Freedom," in *Catholicism and Liberalism: Contributions to American Public Philosophy*, ed. R. Bruce Douglass and David Hollenbach (Cambridge: Cambridge University Press, 1994).

57. Longman and Boshara, *The Next Progressive Era*, 83–87.

58. Michael Sherraden, "Assets and the Social Investment State," in *Equal Shares? Building a Progressive and Coherent Asset-Based Welfare Policy*, ed. Will Paxton (London: Institute for Public Policy Research, 2003), 33.

59. Himes, "Rights of Entitlement," 517.

60. David Hollenbach, S.J., "Common Good," in *The New Dictionary of Catholic Social Thought*, ed. Judith A. Dwyer (Collegeville, MN: Liturgical Press, 1994), 193.

61. Paul VI, *Populorum Progressio* (1967), §19.

62. John Paul II, *Sollicitudo Rei Socialis*, §28.

63. Ibid.

64. Nussbaum, *Frontiers of Justice*, 74.

65. Ibid., 70.

66. Martha C. Nussbaum, "Virtue Revived: Habit, Passion, Reflection in the Aristotelian Tradition," *Times Literary Supplement* 4657 (1992): 10.

67. Nussbaum, "The Good as Discipline, the Good as Freedom," 323–24.

68. Nussbaum, *Women and Human Development*, 81.

69. Ibid., 80.

70. This is one reason why IDA programs require participants to attend classes that teach basic financial management.

71. John P. Caskey, *Fringe Banking: Check-Cashing Outlets, Pawnshops, and the Poor* (New York: Russell Sage Foundation, 1994), 10.

72. Ibid., 2.

73. Ibid., 1.

74. Elizabeth Johnson and Margaret S. Sherraden, *From Financial Literacy to Financial Capability among Youth* (St. Louis: Center for Social Development, Washington University, 2006), 9.

75. Ibid., 10.

76. Anthony Bebbington, "Capitals and Capabilities: A Framework for Analyzing Peasant Viability, Rural Livelihoods and Poverty," *World Development* 27, no. 12 (1999): 2022–23.

Notes to Appendix

1. More recent Catholic social teaching has addressed itself not only to *human* social relations but also to the relationship of human beings to other *non-human* living things and, more generally, to the created order itself. In

other words, it has become increasingly engaged in questions that fall within the purview of environmental ethics. See, for example, John Paul II, *The Ecological Crisis: A Common Responsibility* (Washington, DC: United States Catholic Conference, 1990).

2. Michael J. Schuck divides *modern* Catholic social thought into three main periods: pre-Leonine (1740–1878), Leonine (1879–1958), and post-Leonine (1959–present). He defines modern Catholic social thought as "[m]oral reflection of Roman Catholics on human relations in society since the 18th century" ("Modern Catholic Social Thought," in *The New Dictionary of Catholic Social Thought*, ed. Judith A. Dwyer [Collegeville, MN: Liturgical Press, 1994], 611).

3. Charles E. Curran, *The Catholic Moral Tradition Today: A Synthesis* (Washington, DC: Georgetown University Press, 1999), 197. Cf. Joseph Cardinal Ratzinger: "In the process of assimilating what is really rational and rejecting what only seems to be rational, the whole Church has to play a part. This process cannot be carried out in every detail by an isolated Magisterium, with oracular infallibility. The life and suffering of Christians who profess their faith in the midst of their times has just as important a part to play as the thinking and questioning of the learned, which would have a very hollow ring without the backing of Christian existence, which learns to discern spirits in the travail of everyday life" ("Magisterium of the Church, Faith, Morality," in *Readings in Moral Theology, No. 2*, ed. Charles E. Curran and Richard A. McCormick [New York: Paulist Press, 1980], 186).

4. Aquinas distinguished between the pastoral magisterium of the bishops and pope (*magisterium cathedrae pastoralis*) and the scholarly magisterium of theologians (*magisterium cathedrae magistralis*). See Thomas Aquinas, *Contro Impugnantes Dei cultum et religionem* (An Apology for the Religious Orders), chapter 2 and *Quaestiones quodlibetales* III, q. 4, art 1.

5. In an effort to signal statements made by the hierarchical magisterium from those made by the magisterium of the whole Church, a distinction is sometimes made between Catholic social *teaching* and Catholic social *thought*. Catholic social teaching identifies the writings of the hierarchical magisterium, while Catholic social thought is a general term that applies to the writings of the hierarchy and those of Catholic lay persons. In this book, I do not apply these terms in this way. It should be clear from the context, however, if the phrase is being used in a restrictive way (i.e., to refer to writings of the hierarchical magisterium) or in the more inclusive sense.

6. David J. O'Brien and Thomas A. Shannon, "Roman Catholic Social Teaching," in *Catholic Social Thought: The Documentary Heritage*, ed. David J. O'Brien and Thomas A. Shannon (Maryknoll, NY: Orbis Books, 1992), 6.

7. "[Issues of Catholic social morality] have . . . been explored with the aid of history, social philosophy, political and economic theory, sociology, and

law." As a result, modern Catholic social thought "has been . . . interdisciplinary, exploratory, and wide ranging; it has never been simply a deduction from [fundamental moral theology]" (Schuck, "Modern Catholic Social Thought," 613).

8. Sherraden, "From Research to Policy," 162.

9. Lisa Sowle Cahill, "Justice for Women: Martha Nussbaum and Catholic Social Teaching," in *Transforming Unjust Structures: The Capabilities Approach*, ed. Séverine Deneulin, Mathias Nebel, and Nicholas Sagovsky (Dordrecht: Springer, 2006), 84.

Bibliography

Aquinas, Thomas. "Book One: Commentary on the Nicomachean Ethics." In *Thomas Aquinas: Selected Political Writings*, edited by A. P. D'Entreves, 189–93. Oxford: Basil Blackwell, 1948.

Aristotle. Nicomachean Ethics. Translated by W. D. Ross. Oxford: Clarendon Press, 1905.

———. *Politics. The Complete Works of Aristotle: The Revised Oxford Translation*. Vol. 2. Edited by Jonathan Barnes. Princeton, NJ: Princeton University Press, 1984.

———. *Politics*. In *Introduction to Aristotle*, edited by Richard McKeon, 590–659. Chicago: University of Chicago Press, 1973.

Bane, Mary Jo, and David T. Ellwood. *Welfare Realities: From Rhetoric to Reform*. Cambridge, MA: Harvard University Press, 1994.

Barnes, Martin. "Reaching the Socially Excluded?" In *Asset-Based Welfare and Poverty: Exploring the Case For and Against Asset-Based Welfare Policies*, edited by Claire Kober and Will Paxton, 13–16. London: Institute for Public Policy Research and End Child Poverty, 2002.

Bartels, Larry M. *Unequal Democracy: The Political Economy of the New Gilded Age*. New York and Princeton, NJ: Russell Sage Foundation and Princeton University Press, 2008.

Bebbington, Anthony. "Capitals and Capabilities: A Framework for Analyzing Peasant Viability, Rural Livelihoods and Poverty." *World Development* 27, no. 12 (1999): 2021–44.

Bellah, Robert, Richard Madsen, William M. Sullivan, Ann Swidler, and Steven M. Tipton. *Habits of the Heart: Individualism and Commitment in American Life*. 3rd ed. Berkeley, CA: University of California Press, 1985.

Bernstein, Jared. "Work, Wages and Income Still Matter: Why Asset-Building Isn't Enough." *Shelterforce Online*, no. 128 (2003).

Beverly, Sondra G., and Michael Sherraden. "Institutional Determinants of Savings: Implications for Low-Income Households and Public Policy." *Journal of Socio-Economics* 28, no. 4 (1999): 457–73.

Black, John. *Oxford Dictionary of Economics.* New York: Oxford University Press, 2003.

Bonsor, Jack A. "History, Dogma, and Nature: Reflections on Postmodernism and Theology." *Theological Studies* 55 (1994): 295–313.

Boshara, Ray. "Combating Poverty by Building Assets: Lessons from Around the World." *Pathways* (Spring 2009): 19–23

———. "Poverty Is More Than a Matter of Income." *New York Times*, September 29, 2002, 13.

———. "The Rationale for Assets, Asset-Building Policies, and IDAs for the Poor." In *Building Assets: A Report on the Asset-Development and IDA Field*, edited by Ray Boshara, 5–23. Washington, DC: Corporation for Enterprise Development, 2001.

Boynton, Robert S. "Who Needs Philosophy?" *New York Times*, November 21, 1999.

Bray, Rosemary. *Unafraid of the Dark: A Memoir.* New York: Random House, 1998.

Burman, Leonard, Eric Toder, and Christopher Geissler. "Discussion Paper No. 31: How Big Are Total Individual Tax Expenditures, and Who Benefits from Them?" Washington DC: Urban Institute, 2008.

Burtless, Gary, and Timothy M. Smeeding, "The Level, Trend, and Composition of Poverty." In *Understanding Poverty*, edited by Sheldon H. Danziger and Robert H. Haveman, 27–68. New York and Cambridge, MA: Russell Sage Foundation and Harvard University Press, 2001.

Cahill, Lisa Sowle. *Between the Sexes: Foundations for a Christian Ethics of Sexuality.* Minneapolis, MN: Fortress Press, 1985.

———. "The Catholic Tradition: Religion, Morality, and the Common Good." *Journal of Law and Religion* 5, no. 1 (1987): 75–94.

———. "Justice for Women: Martha Nussbaum and Catholic Social Teaching." In *Transforming Unjust Structures: The Capabilities Approach*, edited by Séverine Deneulin, Mathias Nebel and Nicholas Sagovsky, 83–104. Library of Ethics and Applied Philosophy. Dordrecht: Springer, 2006.

Caskey, John P. *Fringe Banking: Check-Cashing Outlets, Pawnshops, and the Poor.* New York: Russell Sage Foundation, 1994.

Clark, Charles M. A. "Christian Morals and the Competitive System Revisited." *Journal of Economic Issues* 40, no. 2 (2006): 261–75.

Conger, Rand D., Glenn H. Elder, Frederick O. Lorenz, Katherine Conger, Ronald L. Simons, Les B. Whitbeck, Shirley Huck, and Janet N. Melby. "Linking Economic Hardship to Marital Quality and Instability." *Journal of Marriage and the Family* 52 (1990): 643–56.

Conley, Dalton. *Being Black, Living in the Red: Race, Wealth, and Social Policy in America*. Berkeley: University of California Press, 1999.

Corporation for Enterprise Development. "Assets Newsletter." Washington, DC: CFED, 2005.

Cramer, Reid, Alejandra Lopez-Fernandini, and Mark Huelsman. *Presidential Promises: A Review of Campaign Proposals to Promote Savings and Asset Building*. Washington, DC: New America Foundation, 2008.

Curran, Charles E. *The Catholic Moral Tradition Today: A Synthesis*. Washington, DC: Georgetown University Press, 1999.

———. *Catholic Social Teaching, 1891–Present: A Historical, Theological, and Ethical Analysis*. Edited by James F. Keenan. Moral Traditions Series. Washington, DC: Georgetown University Press, 2002.

Deneulin, Séverine, Mathias Nebel, and Nicholas Sagovsky. "Introduction." In *Transforming Unjust Structures: The Capability Approach*, edited by Séverine Deneulin, Mathias Nebel and Nicholas Sagovsky, 1–16. Library of Ethics and Applied Philosophy. Dordrecht: Springer, 2006.

Draut, Tommy, David Callahan, and Corinna Hawkes. *Crossing Divides: New Common Ground on Poverty and Economic Security*. New York: *Demos*, 2002.

Du Bois, W. E. B. "A Negro Nation within a Nation." *Current History* 42 (1935): 265–70.

———. *The Souls of Black Folk*. Greenwich, CT: Fawcett, 1970.

Eagleson, John, and Philip Scharper, eds. *Puebla and Beyond: Documentation and Commentary*. Maryknoll, NY: Orbis Books, 1979.

Edwards, Karen, and Lisa Marie Mason. "State Policy Trends for Individual Development Accounts in the United States." *Social Development Issues* 25 (2003): 118–29.

Ellwood, David T. *Poor Support: Poverty in the American Family*. New York: Basic Books, 1988.

Federal Housing Authority. *Underwriting Manual: Underwriting and Valuation Procedure under Title II of the National Housing Act with Revisions to April 1, 1936*. Washington, DC: FHA, 1936.

Finn, Daniel. "Commentary on *Centesimus Annus* (on the Hundredth Anniversary of *Rerum Novarum*)." In *Modern Catholic Social Teaching: Commentaries and Interpretations*, edited by Kenneth R. Himes, Lisa Sowle Cahill, Charles E. Curran, David Hollenbach, and Thomas A. Shannon, 436–66. Washington, DC: Georgetown University Press, 2004.

Galligan, Richard J., and Stephen J. Bahr. "Economic Well-Being and Marital Stability: Implications for Income Maintenance Programs." *Journal of Marriage and the Family* 40, no. 2 (1978): 283–90.

Gilder, George. *Wealth and Poverty*. New York: Basic Books, 1981.

Gilligan, Carol A. *In a Different Voice: Psychological Theory and Women's Development*. Cambridge, MA: Harvard University Press, 1982.

Greenawalt, Kent. *Private Consciences and Public Reasons*. Oxford: Oxford University Press, 1995.

Gutmann, Amy, and Dennis Thompson. *Democracy and Disagreement*. Cambridge, MA: Belknap Press, 1996.

Harrington, Michael. *The Other America*. New York: Macmillan, 1962.

Haveman, Robert H., and Edward N. Wolff. "Who Are the Asset Poor? Levels, Trends and Composition, 1983–1999." In *Inclusion in Asset Building: Research and Policy Symposium*. St. Louis: Center for Social Development, Washington University, 2000.

Hicks, Douglas A. *Inequality and Christian Ethics*. New Studies in Christian Ethics. Cambridge: Cambridge University Press, 2000.

Himes, Kenneth R. "Rights of Entitlement: A Roman Catholic Perspective." *Notre Dame Journal of Law, Ethics, and Public Policy* 11 (1997): 507–29.

Hobgood, Mary E. "Poor Women, Work and the Catholic Bishops." In *Welfare Policy: Feminist Critiques*, edited by Elizabeth Bounds, Pamela Brubaker, and Mary E. Hobgood, 175–200. Cleveland: Pilgrim Press, 1999.

Hollenbach, David, S.J. "Afterword: A Community of Freedom." In *Catholicism and Liberalism: Contributions to American Public Philosophy*, edited by R. Bruce Douglass and David Hollenbach, 323–43. Cambridge: Cambridge University Press, 1994.

———. "Christian Social Ethics after the Cold War." *Theological Studies* 53, no. 1 (1992): 75–95.

———. *Claims in Conflict: Retrieving and Renewing the Catholic Human Rights Tradition*. New York: Paulist Press, 1979.

———. "Common Good." In *The New Dictionary of Catholic Social Thought*, edited by Judith A. Dwyer, 192–97. Collegeville, MN: Liturgical Press, 1994.

———. *The Common Good and Christian Ethics*. Edited by Robin Gill. Vol. 22. New Studies in Christian Ethics. Cambridge: Cambridge University Press, 2002.

Howard, Christopher. *The Hidden Welfare State: Tax Expenditures and Social Policy in the United States*. Princeton, NJ: Princeton University Press, 1997.

Hungerford, Thomas L. *Tax Expenditures: Trends and Critiques*. Congressional Research Service. Library of Congress, 2006. 1–24.

John XXIII. 1961. *Mater et Magistra* [1961]. In *Catholic Social Thought: The Documentary Heritage*, edited by David J. O'Brien and Thomas A. Shannon, 84–128. Maryknoll, NY: Orbis Books, 1992.

———. *Pacem in Terris* [1963]. In *Catholic Social Thought: The Documentary Heritage*, edited by David J. O'Brien and Thomas A. Shannon, 131–59. Maryknoll, NY: Orbis Books, 1992.

John Paul II. *Centesimus Annus* [1991]. In *Catholic Social Thought: The Documentary Heritage*, edited by David J. O'Brien and Thomas A. Shannon, 439–88. Maryknoll, NY: Orbis Books, 1992.

————. *The Ecological Crisis: A Common Responsibility*. Washington, D.C.: United States Catholic Conference, 1990.

————. *Laborem Exercens* [1981]. In *Catholic Social Thought: The Documentary Heritage*, edited by David J. O'Brien and Thomas Shannon, 350–92. Maryknoll, NY: Orbis, 1992.

————. *Sollicitudo Rei Socialis* [1987]. In *Catholic Social Thought: The Documentary Heritage*, edited by David J. O'Brien and Thomas A. Shannon, 395–436. Maryknoll, NY: Orbis Books, 1992.

Johnson, Elizabeth, and Margaret S. Sherraden. *From Financial Literacy to Financial Capability among Youth*. St. Louis: Center for Social Development, Washington University, 2006. 1–34.

Kahneman, Daniel, and Amos Tversky. "Prospect Theory: An Analysis of Decision under Risk." *Econometrica* 47, no. 2 (1979): 263–91.

Kant, Immanuel. *Foundations of the Metaphysics of Morals*. Translated by Lewis White Beck. 2nd ed. Princeton, NJ: Prentice Hall, 1989.

Kaplan, Jonathan, and Andrew Valls. "Housing Discrimination as a Basis for Black Reparations." *Public Affairs Quarterly* 21, no. 3 (2007): 255–73.

Kelsey, David F. *The Uses of Scripture in Recent Theology*. Minneapolis: Fortress Press, 1975.

Kohlberg, Lawrence. *Essays in Moral Development: The Psychology of Moral Development*. Vol. 2. San Francisco: Harper & Row, 1984.

Latin American Episcopate. "Puebla Final Document." In *Puebla and Beyond: Documentation and Commentary*, edited by John Eagleson and Philip Scharper, 123–288. Maryknoll, NY: Orbis Books, 1979.

Leo XIII. *Rerum Novarum* [1891]. In *Catholic Social Thought: The Documentary Heritage*, edited by David J. O'Brien and Thomas A. Shannon, 14–39. Maryknoll, NY: Orbis Books, 1992.

Lerman, Robert I., and Signe-Mary McKernan. "Benefits and Consequences of Holding Assets." In *Asset Building and Low-Income Families*, edited by Signe-Mary McKernan and Michael Sherraden, 175–206. Washington, DC: Urban Institute Press, 2008.

Levinger, G., and O. Moles, eds. *Divorce and Separation: Contexts, Causes, and Consequences*. New York: Basic Books, 1979.

Lind, Michael. "The Small Holder Society." *Harvard Law & Policy Review* 1 (2007): 143–60.

Lindberg, Carter. *Beyond Charity: Reformation Initiatives for the Poor*. Minneapolis: Fortress Press, 1993.

Locke, John. *The Second Treatise of Government*. Edited by Thomas P. Peardon. Indianapolis: Bobbs-Merrill, 1960.

Loke, Vernon, and Michael Sherraden. "Building Assets from Birth: A Global Comparison of Child Development Account Policies." *International Journal of Social Welfare* 18 (2009): 119–29.

Longman, Phillip, and Ray Boshara. *The Next Progressive Era: A Blueprint for Broad Prosperity.* Sausalito, CA: PoliPoint Press, 2009.

Losby, Jan L., and Jill R. Robinson. *Michigan IDA Partnership: Year Three Program Evaluation Report.* Washington, DC: ISED Solutions, 2004.

Lustig, B. Andrew. "Property and Justice in the Modern Encyclical Literature." *Harvard Theological Review* 83, no. 4 (1990): 415–46.

Lyotard, Jean-Francois. *The Postmodern Condition: A Report on Knowledge.* Manchester: Manchester University Press, 1984.

Maier, Norman R. F. "Reasoning in Humans II: The Solution of a Problem and Its Appearance in Consciousness." *Journal of Comparative Psychology* 12 (1931): 181–94.

Massey, Douglas S. "Race, Class, and Markets: Social Policy in the 21st Century." In *Poverty and Inequality,* edited by David B. Grusky and Ravi Kanbur, 117–32. Studies in Social Inequality. Stanford, CA: Stanford University Press, 2006.

Massey, Douglas S., and Nancy A. Denton. *American Apartheid: Segregation and the Making of the Underclass.* Cambridge, MA: Harvard University Press, 1993.

Mead, Lawrence, ed. *The New Paternalism: Supervisory Approaches to Poverty.* Washington DC: Brookings Institution Press, 1997.

———. *The New Politics of Poverty.* New York: Basic Books, 1992.

Midgley, James. "Asset Based Policy in Historical and International Perspective." In *Inclusion in the American Dream: Assets, Poverty, and Public Policy,* edited by Michael Sherraden, 42–58. Oxford: Oxford University Press, 2006.

Mishel, Lawrence, Jared Bernstein, and Heidi Shierholz. *The State of Working America, 2008/2009.* Ithaca, NY: Cornell University Press, 2009.

Moore, Amanda, Sondra Beverly, Mark Schreiner, Michael Sherraden, and Margaret Lombe. *Saving, IDA Programs, and Effects of IDAs: A Survey of Participants.* St. Louis: Center of Social Development, Washington University, 2001.

Moses, Sarah. "A Just Society for the Elderly: The Importance of Justice as Participation." *Notre Dame Journal of Law, Ethics, and Public Policy* 21 (2007).

Murray, Charles. *Losing Ground: American Social Policy 1950–1980.* New York: Basic Books, 1984.

Nam, Yunju, Caroline Ratcliffe, and Signe-Mary McKernan. "Effects of Asset Tests and IDA Programs." In *Asset Building and Low-Income Families,* edited by Signe-Mary McKernan and Michael Sherraden, 153–73. Washington, DC: Urban Institute Press, 2008.

Nam, Yunju, Jin Huang, and Michael Sherraden. "Asset Definitions." In *Asset Building and Low-Income Families,* edited by Signe-Mary McKernan and Michael Sherraden, 1–31. Washington, DC: Urban Institute Press, 2008.

Naraya, Uma. "Contesting Cultures: 'Westernization,' Respect for Cultures, and Third World-Feminists." In *Dislocating Cultures: Identities, Traditions, and Third World Feminism*, 1–40. New York: Routledge, 1997.

National Catholic War Council. "Program for Social Reconstruction in the Marketplace." In *American Catholic Social Teaching*, edited by Thomas J. Massaro and Thomas A. Shannon, 50–58. Collegeville, MN: Michael Glazier Books, 1919.

National Conference of Catholic Bishops. *Brothers and Sisters to Us: Pastoral Letter on Racism*. Washington, DC: National Conference of Catholic Bishops, 1979.

———. *Economic Justice for All: Pastoral Letter on Catholic Social Teaching and the U.S. Economy*. Washington, DC: United States Catholic Conference, 1986.

North, Douglass. *Structure and Change in Economic History*. New York: W. W. Norton, 1981.

Nussbaum, Martha C. "Aristotelian Social Democracy." In *Liberalism and the Good*, edited by R. Bruce Douglass, Gerald M. Mara, and Henry S. Richardson, 203–52. New York and London: Routledge, 1990.

———. "Aristotle, Politics, and Human Capabilities: A Response to Antony, Arneson, Charlesworth, and Mulgan." *Ethics* 111 (2000): 102–40.

———. *Frontiers of Justice*. Cambridge, MA: Belknap Press of Harvard University, 2007.

———. "The Good as Discipline, the Good as Freedom." In *Ethics of Consumption: The Good Life, Justice, and Global Stewardship*, edited by David A. Crocker and Toby Linden. Lanham, MD: Rowman & Littlefield, 1998.

———. "Human Capabilities, Female Human Beings." In *Women, Culture, and Development: A Study of Human Capabilities (a Study Prepared for the World Institute for Development Economics Research [Wider] of the United Nations University Wider Studies in Development Economics)*, edited by Martha C. Nussbaum and Jonathan Glover, 61–104. Oxford and New York: Clarendon Press and Oxford University Press, 1995.

———. "Human Functioning and Social Justice: In Defense of Aristotelian Essentialism." *Political Theory* 20, no. 2 (1992): 202–46.

———. "Non-Relative Virtues: An Aristotelian Approach." In *The Quality of Life*, edited by Martha C. Nussbaum and Amartya Sen, 242–69. Oxford: Clarendon Press, 1993.

———. "Non-Relative Virtues: An Aristotelian Approach." In *Ethical Theory: Character and Virtue*, edited by Peter A. French, Theodore Uebling, Jr. and Howard K. Wettstein, 32–53. Midwest Studies in Philosophy. Notre Dame, IN: University of Notre Dame, 1988.

———. "Poverty and Human Functioning: Capabilities as Fundamental Entitlements." In *Poverty and Inequality*, edited by David B. Grusky and Ravi

Kanbur, 47–75. Studies in Social Inequality. Stanford, CA: Stanford University Press, 2006.

———. "Public Philosophy and International Feminism." *Ethics* 108 (1998): 762–96.

———. "Religion and Women's Human Rights." In *Religion and Contemporary Liberalism*, edited by Paul J. Weithman, 93–137. Notre Dame, IN: University of Notre Dame Press, 1997.

———. "Social Justice and Universalism: In Defense of an Aristotelian Account of Human Functioning." *Modern Philology* 90, no. Supplement (1993): S46–S73.

———. "Virtue Revived: Habit, Passion, Reflection in the Aristotelian Tradition." *Times Literary Supplement* 4657 (1992): 9–11.

———. *Women and Human Development: The Capabilities Approach.* New York: Cambridge University Press, 2000.

Nussbaum, Martha C., and Jonathan Glover, eds. *Women, Culture, and Development. A Study of Human Capabilities.* Studies in Development Economics. New York: Oxford, 1996.

Obama, Barack. "A More Perfect Union." *New York Times*, March 18, 2008.

O'Brien, David J., and Thomas A. Shannon, eds. *Catholic Social Thought: The Documentary Heritage.* Maryknoll, NY: Orbis Books, 1992.

———. "Roman Catholic Social Teaching." In *Catholic Social Thought: The Documentary Heritage*, edited by David J. O'Brien and Thomas A. Shannon, 1–7. Maryknoll, NY: Orbis Books, 1992.

Oliver, Melvin, and Thomas Shapiro. *Black Wealth/White Wealth: A New Perspective on Racial Inequality.* New York: Routledge, 1995.

O'Neill, William J., S.J. "Poverty in the United States." In *Resources for Social and Cultural Analysis: Reading the Signs of the Times*, edited by T. Howland Sanks and John A. Coleman, 68–77. New York: Paulist Press, 1993.

Organization for Economic Cooperation and Development. *Asset Building and the Escape from Poverty: A New Welfare Policy Debate.* Paris: OECD, 2003.

Oubre, Claude F. *Forty Acres and a Mule: The Freedmen's Bureau and Black Land Ownership.* Baton Rouge: Louisiana State University Press, 1978.

Paul VI. *Populorum Progressio* [1967]. In *Catholic Social Thought: The Documentary Heritage*, edited by David J. O'Brien and Thomas A. Shannon, 240–62. Maryknoll, NY: Orbis Books, 1992.

Pavetti, Ladonna A. "Welfare Policy in Transition: Redefining the Social Contract for Poor Citizen Families with Children and for Immigrants." In *Understanding Poverty*, edited by Sheldon H. Danziger and Robert H. Haveman, 229–77. New York and Cambridge, MA: Russell Sage Foundation and Harvard University Press, 2001.

Perry, Michael J. "Neutral Politics." In *Love and Power*, 8–28. Oxford and New York: Oxford University Press, 1993

————. *Under God? Religious Faith and Liberal Democracy.* Cambridge: Cambridge University Press, 2003.

Pius XI. *Quadragesimo Anno* [1931]. In *Catholic Social Thought: The Documentary Heritage*, edited by David J. O'Brien and Thomas A. Shannon, 42–79. Maryknoll, NY: Orbis Books, 1992.

Pius XII. "The Internal Orders of States and People." Christmas Broadcast Message. 1942.

Pope, Stephen J. "Proper and Improper Partiality and the Preferential Option for the Poor." *Theological Studies* 54, no. 2 (1993): 242–71.

Putnam, Robert. *Bowling Alone: The Collapse and Revival of the American Community.* New York: Simon and Schuster, 2001.

Ratzinger, Joseph, Cardinal. "Magisterium of the Church, Faith, Morality." In *Readings in Moral Theology, No. 2*, edited by Charles E. Curran and Richard A. McCormick. New York: Paulist Press, 1980.

Rawls, John. "The Idea of an Overlapping Consensus." *Oxford Journal for Legal Studies* 7, no. 1 (Spring 1987): 1–25.

————. *Political Liberalism.* New York: Columbia University Press, 1993. Reprint, 1996.

————. "Preface for the French Edition of a Theory of Justice" [1987]. In *John Rawls: Collected Papers*, edited by Samuel Freeman, 415–20. Cambridge, MA: Harvard University Press, 1999.

————. *A Theory of Justice.* Revised edition. Oxford: Oxford University Press, 1999.

Rorty, Richard. "The Priority of Democracy to Philosophy." In *Prospects for a Common Morality*, edited by Gene Outka and John P. Reeder, 254–78. Princeton, NJ: Princeton University Press, 1992.

Rusk, David. "Social Change Strategies for the Future of Metropolitan Areas." In *Living the Catholic Social Tradition: Introduction and Overview*, edited by Kathleen Maas Weigert and Alexia K. Kelley, 15–39. Lanham, MD: Rowman & Littlefield, 2005.

Rutherford, Stuart. *The Poor and Their Money.* New York: Oxford University Press, 2000.

Scanlon, Edward, and Deborah Page-Adams. "Effects of Asset Holding on Neighborhoods, Families, and Children: A Review of the Research." In *Building Assets: A Report on the Asset-Development and IDA Field*, edited by Ray Boshara, 25–50. Washington, DC: Corporation for Enterprise Development, 2001.

Schram, Sanford F. *Welfare Discipline: Discourse, Governance, and Globalization.* Philadelphia: Temple University Press, 2006.

Schreiner, Mark, and Michael Sherraden. *Can the Poor Save? Saving & Asset Building in Individual Development Accounts.* New Brunswick and London: Transaction, 2007.

Schreiner, Mark, Margaret Clancy, and Michael Sherraden. *Final Report: Saving Performance in the American Dream Demonstration: A National Demonstration of Individual Development Accounts.* St. Louis: Center for Social Development, Washington University, 2002.

Schreiner, Mark, Michael Sherraden, Margaret Clancy, Lissa Johnson, Jami Curley, Min Zhan, Sondra G. Beverly, and Michal Grinstein-Weiss. "Assets and the Poor: Evidence from Individual Development Accounts." In *Inclusion in the American Dream: Assets, Poverty, and Public Policy*, edited by Michael Sherraden, 185–215. New York and Oxford: Oxford University Press, 2005.

Schuck, Michael J. "Modern Catholic Social Thought." In *The New Dictionary of Catholic Social Thought*, edited by Judith A. Dwyer, 611–32. Collegeville, MN: Liturgical Press, 1994.

Segundo, Juan Luis. *Theology and the Church: A Response to Cardinal Ratzinger and a Warning to the Whole Church.* Minneapolis: Winston Press, 1985.

Seidman, Laurence S. "Assets and the Tax Code." In *Assets for the Poor: The Benefits of Spreading Asset Ownership*, edited by Thomas Shapiro and Edward N. Wolff, 324–56. New York: Russell Sage Foundation, 2001.

Sen, Amartya. *Development as Freedom.* New York: Anchor, 2000.

Shain, Barry Alan. *The Myth of American Individualism.* Princeton, NJ: Princeton University Press, 1996.

Shanks, Trina Williams. "The Homestead Act: A Major Asset-Building Policy in American History." In *Inclusion in the American Dream: Assets, Poverty, and Public Policy*, edited by Michael Sherraden, 20–41. New York: Oxford University Press, 2005.

Shapiro, Thomas. *The Hidden Cost of Being African American: How Wealth Perpetuates Inequality.* New York: Oxford University Press, 2004.

Shapiro, Thomas M., and Edward N. Wolff. *Assets for the Poor: The Benefits of Spreading Asset Ownership.* The Ford Foundation Series on Asset Building. New York: Russell Sage Foundation, 2001.

Sherraden, Michael. "Asset-Building Policy and Programs for the Poor." In *Assets for the Poor: The Benefits of Spreading Asset Ownership*, edited by Thomas Shapiro and Edward N. Wolff, 302–23. New York: Russell Sage Foundation, 2001.

———. *Assets and the Poor: A New American Welfare Policy.* Armonk, NY: M. E. Sharp, 1991.

———. "Assets and the Social Investment State." In *Equal Shares? Building a Progressive and Coherent Asset-Based Welfare Policy*, edited by Will Paxton, 28–41. London: Institute for Public Policy Research, 2003.

———. "From a Social Welfare State to a Social Investment State." In *Asset-Based Welfare and Poverty: Exploring the Case For and Against Asset-Based Welfare Policies*, edited by C. Kober and W. Paxton, 5–8. London: Institute for Public Policy Research and End Child Poverty, 2002.

————. "From a Social Welfare State to a Social Investment State." *Shelterforce Online*, no. 128 (2003). Available online at http://www.nhi.org/online/issues/128/socialinvest.html.

————. "From Research to Policy: Lessons from Individual Development Accounts." *The Journal of Consumer Affairs* 34, no. 2 (2000): 159–81.

————. *IDAs and Asset-Building Policy: Lessons and Directions.* St. Louis: Washington University, 2008.

————, ed. *Inclusion in the American Dream: Assets, Poverty, and Public Policy.* New York: Oxford University Press, 2005.

————. "Individual Development Accounts." *The Entrepreneurial Economy Review* 8, no. 5 (1989): 1–22.

Shuman, Howard E. *Politics and the Budget: The Struggle between the President and Congress.* Englewood Cliffs, NJ: Prentice Hall, 1984.

Simon, William E., and Michael Novak. *Liberty and Justice for All: Report on the Final Draft (June 1986) of the U.S. Catholic Bishops' Pastoral Letter "Economic Justice for All".* Notre Dame, IN: Brownson Institute, 1986.

Smith, Adam. *An Inquiry into the Nature and Causes of the Wealth of Nations.* Edited by C. J. Bullock. Harvard Classics. New York: P. F. Collier & Son, 1909.

Straus, S. W., and Rollin Kirby. *History of the Thrift Movement.* Philadelphia: Lippincott, 1920.

Sunshine, Robert A. *The Budget and Economic Outlook: Fiscal Years 2009 to 2019.* Report to Senate Committee on the Budget, 111th Congress, 1st sess., 2009. 1–47.

Thaler, Richard H., and Cass R. Sunstein. *Nudge: Improving Decisions about Health, Wealth, and Happiness.* New Haven, CT and London: Yale University Press, 2008.

Tversky, Amos, and Daniel Kahneman. "The Framing of Decision and the Psychology of Choice." *Science* 211, no. 4481 (1981): 454–58.

Tyagi, Amelia Warren. "*Marketplace* Commentary on Sub-Prime Mortgage Crisis." In *Marketplace*, edited by Kai Ryssdal. American Public Media, 2009.

Vatican Council, Second. *Gaudium et Spes* [1965]. In *Catholic Social Thought: The Documentary Heritage*, edited by David J. O'Brien and Thomas A. Shannon, 166–237. Maryknoll, NY: Orbis Books, 1992.

Will, George. "Folly and the Fed." *Washington Post*, August 16, 2007. A15.

Williams, Trina R. *Asset-Building Policy as a Response to Wealth Inequality: Drawing Implications from the Homestead Act.* St. Louis: Center for Social Development, Washington University, 2003.

Woo, Lillian, and David Buchholz. *Subsidies for Assets: A New Look at the Federal Budget, Federal Reserve System.* Washington, DC: Corporation for Enterprise Development, 2007.

Index

Adams, John, 80–81
African Americans
  housing discrimination against, 86,
    96–98
  loan discrimination against, 86,
    98–99
  during New Deal, 94–97
  Obama on discrimination against,
    86–87
  during Reconstruction, 88–94
  wealth disparities with whites, 4,
    81–82, 87
Aid to Families with Dependent
  Children (AFDC), 9, 95
American Dream Demonstration
  (ADD), 108, 109
American Opportunity Tax Credit,
  113
American Stakeholder Account
  (ASA), 111
America Saving for Personal
  Investment, Retirement, and
  Education Act (ASPIRE), 111
Aquinas, Thomas, 47–48, 127, 154n4
Aristotle, 47–48, 66–67, 143n14
asset accumulation. *See* saving and
  asset accumulation

asset-building approach
  and aggregate economic measur-
    ing, 74
  and capabilities approach, 77
  and Catholic social thought, 32, 43,
    51, 54–59
  as distinct from income-bolstering
    approach, 12, 15, 16, 55–56, 63
  need for paradigm shift toward, 13,
    16, 103, 109–10
  and personal efficacy, 16, 79
asset-building policies, 4, 56, 110–11,
  116–26
  American Dream Demonstration,
    108, 109
  American Opportunity Tax Credit,
    113
  American Stakeholder Account, 111
  America Saving for Personal
    Investment, Retirement, and
    Education Act, 111
  Assets for Independence Act, 112,
    151n33
  Child Savings Account, 110–11,
    119, 151n27
  individual development accounts,
    107–10, 112, 113, 120, 150n11

asset-building policies (*cont.*)
  political viability of, 112–14
  possible perils of, 114–16
  during Reconstruction era, 88–89,
    146n7
  regressive application of, 18–23,
    104–5, 114–15, 120
  Savings for Working Families Act,
    113
  Temporary Assistance for Needy
    Families, 108, 150n15
assets. *See* ownership of assets
Assets for Independence Act, 112,
  151n33
Augustine, 55
Australia, 113–14

banking system, 98–99
Bebbington, Anthony, 126
behavioral economics, 106–7
Benton, Thomas Hart, 81
Bernstein, Jared, 115
Bill and Melinda Gates Foundation, 114
bipartisanship, 112
"black codes," 98
Bonsor, Jack, 65
Boshara, Ray, 106–7, 119
Bram, Henry, 90–91
Bray, Rosemary, 17–18
Buchholz, David, 20

Canada, 111, 113–14
capabilities approach
  advantages and justifications of,
    62–63
  and asset building for poor, 3–4,
    62, 77
  and Catholic social thought, 2, 4,
    38–39, 62–63
  formulation and definition of,
    61–62, 142n1
  on human dignity, 62, 72, 122

on human freedom, 83, 123
on human good, 67–68
and human rights theories, 73
on human values, 62, 66, 67, 68,
  71–72, 86, 144n30
and human well-being, 74–75, 76,
  123
identification and interrelation of
  capabilities, 68–74, 76
liberals and, 73–74
limitation/capability distinction
  in, 70
on measuring quality of life, 74–75,
  134n23
Michael Sherraden on, 63, 142n6
moral vision of, 3, 117, 122, 123,
  125–26
normative contributions of, 122–26
on ownership of assets, 75–76,
  125–26
and postmodernist thought, 64–66
on social justice, 61–62, 63, 125
on social nature of the individual,
  71, 124
See also Nussbaum, Martha
capitalism, 100, 114, 121
  Catholic social thought on, 30–31,
    36
Catholic social thought
  and capabilities approach, 2, 4,
    38–39, 62–63
  on capitalism, 30–31, 36
  and Catholic social *teaching,* 127,
    154n5
  on charity, 55
  on common good, 49–50, 85, 117,
    120–21, 131
  on community, 46–47, 119
  contributions of to asset-building
    approach, 3, 54–59
  on discrimination, 50, 85
  and environmental ethics, 163n1

on full participation in society,
47–48, 49, 51, 53, 57, 118
on human dignity, 44–46, 53, 61,
86, 117–18, 152n54
on human freedom, 44, 46, 48–49,
50–51, 117, 118–19
on humans as historical beings, 86
interdisciplinary nature of, 129,
154n7
John Paul II and, 36–40
John XXIII and, 33–35
Latin American bishops and, 50, 52
Leo XIII and, 26, 27–30, 137n10,
137n13
listing of documents of, 129, 130
magisterium of, 128–29, 154nn3–5
and non-Catholics, 44, 56, 58, 131
normative contributions of,
117–22
on ownership, 26–30, 31, 34–35,
37–38, 42–43, 57, 86, 126, 136n4
papal encyclicals in, 26, 27, 30, 38,
127, 128, 129
Paul VI and, 35–36
on preferential option for poor,
52–54, 117, 118–19
and public policy, 2, 3, 42, 43, 56,
117
Quadragesimo Anno (Pius XI),
30–33
on saving and asset accumulation,
32, 43, 51, 54–59
Second Vatican Council and, 45–46,
49, 51, 129, 131
social justice tradition of, 2, 32, 33,
43, 63, 117, 119, 126
on social nature of the individual,
39, 44, 46–49, 53, 117, 118,
152n54
three periods of, 127, 154n2
U.S. bishops and, 25, 39–43, 45, 47,
48, 51, 53

on wages, 28, 30, 31–32, 35
on work, 57
Center for Social Development,
Washington University, 114
Centesimus Annus (John Paul II), 37
charity, 1
Christian primacy to, 52
overemphasis on, 55, 119
check-cashing outlets (CCOs),
124–25
Child Savings Account (CSA), 110–11,
119, 151n27
Child Trust Fund (CTF), 110, 111
Clark, Charles, 8
Clement of Alexandria, 54–55
Clinton, Bill, 112
Colombia, 113–14
common good, 86
Catholic social thought on, 49–50,
85, 117, 120–21, 131
planetary, 121
community
in Catholic social thought, 46–47,
119
liberalism and, 49
"Community of Freedom, A"
(Hollenbach), 118–19
Conley, Dalton, 94, 100
conservatives
on mortgage crisis, 99, 149n51
on poverty and welfare, 9–10,
133n16
consumerism, 119, 121
and asset-building policy, 114, 116,
122
consumption
and definition of poverty, 7–9,
12–13, 143n6
excessive and conspicuous, 63, 114,
116, 121–22, 123
and public policy, 1, 21, 23, 76–77
and savings behavior, 3, 22

Corporation for Enterprise
    Development, 114
cross-cultural ethic, 64, 65, 68, 70
Curran, Charles, 128, 137n10

Demos, 114
dependency, 1, 9, 116
discrimination
    in banking system, 86, 98–99
    based on class, 102, 104
    Catholic social thought on, 50, 85
    cost of, 100–102
    in housing, 96–99, 101
    under New Deal, 94–97
    Obama on, 86–87
    public policy fostering, 18–22, 87,
        101–2, 104–5, 120
    social consequences of, 50, 85
    in Social Security, 95–96
    statistics on, 100–101
    and universalist principles, 65, 66
    and wealth gap, 87, 100–101, 103,
        149n1
    See also inequality
Du Bois, W. E. B., 92, 93, 94–95

Economic Justice for All (National
    Conference of Catholic Bishops),
    25, 40–43, 45, 47, 48, 51, 53
Ellwood, David, 10, 133n16
Emancipation Proclamation, 89
entitlements, 21–22, 62, 117
environment
    and capabilities for good life, 72, 77
    and Catholic social teaching, 153n1
    denigration of, 116, 121
Exodus, 46, 52

Federal Housing Authority (FHA), 95,
    96–97, 105, 148n35
financial literacy, 124–25
financial services industry, 124–25

Finn, Daniel, 37
focus and specialization, 78–79
food stamps, 1, 12, 135n38
Ford Foundation, 114
401(k) plans, 23, 106, 113
Freedmen's Bank, 93–94
Freedmen's Bureau, 92–93
freedom
    and capabilities, 83, 123, 134n23
    in Catholic social thought, 44, 46,
        48–49, 50–51, 53, 117, 118–19
    and demands of community, 49
    and ownership of assets, 50–51, 80

Gaudium et Spes (Second Vatican
    Council), 51
G. I. Bill, 95, 105
good life, 66, 68–74
    and capabilities/limitations distinc-
        tion, 70
    excessive wealth as impediment to,
        63
    list of capabilities for, 71–72
    and public policy, 69
    See also common good
Gorbachev, Mikhail, 139n51
Gospels, 52
Grameen Bank, 114
Great Depression, 94, 95
Greenspan, Alan, 113
Gross National Product (GNP),
    74–75, 134n23

Harrington, Michael, 21
Himes, Kenneth, 118, 120
Hollenbach, David, 38, 40, 49, 118–19
home ownership
    discrimination in, 96–99, 101
    as goal, 115
    and household stability, 16, 77–78
    and mortgage crisis, 57–58, 99–100,
        116, 149n51

and political stability, 80
tax subsidies for, 1, 21
Home Owner's Loan Corporation
 (HOLC), 95, 96
Homestead Act, 88–89, 94, 105
Howard, Christopher, 21
Howard, Oliver, 90, 92
human beings
 and animals, 69
 capabilities approach to, 62, 65, 66,
  67, 68, 71–72, 86, 144n30
 as historical beings, 65, 86
 interdependency of, 39, 46, 64, 119,
  129
 material needs of, 31, 44, 48, 51,
  61, 86
 and private property, 38
 and social institutions, 74, 124
 social nature of, 39, 44, 46–49, 53,
  71, 86, 117, 118, 124, 152n54
human capital, 16, 78
human dignity
 and capabilities approach, 62, 72,
  122
 in Catholic social thought, 44–46,
  53, 61, 86, 117–18, 152n54
 and participation in society, 57
 poverty's undermining of, 50
Hungary, 113–14

income
 and assets, 14–15, 16, 55–56
 disruptions in, 77–78
 as measurement of poverty and
  well-being, 1, 7–8, 12
 and wealth, 81
income-bolstering approach
 aim of, 9
 as distinct from asset-building
  approach, 12, 15, 16, 55–56, 63
 entitlements, 21–22, 62, 117
 food stamps, 1, 12, 135n38

Social Security, 18, 21, 33–34
 as strategy to reduce poverty, 11, 12,
  15–16
individual development accounts
 (IDAs), 107–10, 112, 113, 120,
  150n11
individualism
 excessive, 35, 115, 120
 "rugged," 6, 44
individual retirement accounts
 (IRAs), 107–8, 113
Indonesia, 113–14
inductive approach, 76–77
industrialization, 35
inequality
 Paul VI on, 35–36
 Pius XI on, 30–31, 32–33
 public policies reinforcing, 18–23,
  104–5, 120
 of wealth in U.S., 1, 4, 18–24, 41,
  81–82, 87, 100–101, 103, 149n1
 See also discrimination
*Inquiry into the Nature and Causes of
 Wealth of Nations, An* (Smith),
 78–79
intellectual property, 39–40

John Paul II
 on being/having distinction,
  121–22
 on ownership, 36–40
 on preferential option for poor,
  52–53
Johnson, Andrew, 89–90, 91–92
Johnson, Elizabeth, 125
John XXIII, 33–35, 49, 50–51

Kaplan, Jonathan, 101
Kerry, John, 112

Laborum Exercens (John Paul II), 37
land grant colleges, 146n7

Lang, Eugene, 82
Latin American bishops, 50, 52
Leo XIII, 26, 27–30, 127–28, 137n10,
    137n13
liberals
    and capabilities approach, 73–74
    income-based approach of, 10–11
    on individual freedom and com-
        munity, 49
    and postmodernism, 64
liberation theology, 36, 139n52
Liberty and Justice for All (Simon and
    Novak), 142n112
Lieberman, Joseph, 113
Lincoln, Abraham, 88, 89
Lind, Michael, 80–81
Lindberg, Carter, 54–55
Locke, John, 137n10
Loke, Vernon, 110
Longman, Phillip, 111, 119
Lustig, Andrew, 29

Maier, Norman, 5–7
Marxism, 31, 74
    and liberation theology, 36, 139n52
Medicare and Medicaid, 18, 21
minimum wage, 1, 11, 12, 33, 41–42
Morrill, Justin Smith, 146n7
Morrill Act
    First, 146n7
    Second, 146n7
mortgage crisis, 57–58, 99–100, 116,
    149n51
Moses, Sarah, 116
Moultrie, Ishmael, 90–91

National Association of Real Estate
    Brokers, 97–98
National Conference of Catholic
    Bishops (NCCB)
    Economic Justice for All, 25, 40–43,
        45, 47, 48, 51, 53

Native Americans, 87
New American Foundation, 114
New Deal, 94–97
New Zealand, 113–14
North, Douglass, 105–6
Novak, Michael, 142n112
Nussbaum, Martha
    on Aristotelian approach, 66–67, 73
    and Catholic social thought, 2,
        4, 83
    and human freedom, 83
    on human well-being and good, 3,
        63, 67–68, 74–75, 78, 123
    identification of human capabili-
        ties, 68–74
    moral vision of, 3, 117, 122
    on participation in society, 61
    philosophical approach of, 134n23,
        142n1
    on practical reason, 70, 71, 73, 78,
        79, 82
    on social nature of the individual,
        71, 124
    on universalism, 65, 66
    See also capabilities approach

Obama, Barack, 86–87, 112–13
Oliver, Melvin, 16, 99, 102
O'Neill, William, 45
Organization for Economic
    Cooperation and Development
    (OECD), 80
ownership of assets
    capabilities approach to, 75–76,
        125–26
    in Catholic social thought, 26–30,
        31, 34–35, 37–38, 42–43, 57, 86,
        126, 136n4
    definitions of assets, 134n24
    employee partnerships in, 31–32,
        33, 35, 51, 138n32
    and freedom, 50–51, 80

and household stability, 16, 77–78
and income, 14–15, 16, 55–56
intergenerational effects of, 81
John Paul II on, 37–38
John XXIII on, 34–35
labor-based theory of, 137n10
Leo XIII on, 27–30
as "natural right," 28, 31, 37
and orientation toward future, 82
Paul VI on, 35
and political participation, 80–81
as protection against income disruption, 77–78
psychosocial effects of, 16–18, 57, 79, 82, 109
and quality of life, 91
responsibilities of, 30, 37, 138n22
and risk taking, 79
as road to participation in society, 25, 42, 49, 51, 53, 57
and social influence, 79–80
See also asset-building approach; asset-building policies
"ownership society," 43

Page-Adams, Deborah, 16
partiality, 53–54
participation in society
asset ownership as road to, 25, 42, 49, 51, 53, 57
in Catholic social thought, 47–48, 49, 51, 53, 57, 118
political, 72
Paul VI, 35–36, 121
Pavetti, Ladonna A., 133n14
pawnshops, 124, 125
personal efficacy, 16, 79
Personal Responsibility and Work Opportunity Reconciliation Act (PRWORA), 9–11
Peru, 113–14
Pew Charitable Trusts, 114

Pitts, Joe, 113
Pius XI, 30–33, 50
Poland, 36
Politics (Aristotle), 66, 143n14
Pope, Stephen, 53–54
postmodernism, 64–67
poverty
asset-building approach to, 1–2, 12–18, 82–83
and charity, 1, 52, 55, 119
conservative perspective on, 9–10, 133n16
definitions of, 1, 7–9, 12, 134n23
and dependency, 1, 9, 116
income-bolstering approach to, 8, 11, 12, 13–16
in Latin America, 50
need for paradigm shift in policy toward, 13, 16, 103, 109–10
poverty line in U.S., 8–9, 11
preferential option for poor, 52–54, 117, 119–20
relationship of wealthy and poor, 55
social-psychological stresses of, 17–18, 77–78
statistics on, 11
and welfare system, 17, 24
See also asset-building approach; public policy toward poverty
practical reason, 70, 71, 73, 78, 79, 82, 125
preferential option for poor, 52–54, 117, 119–20
reservations about, 53
private property. *See* ownership of assets
public policy toward poverty
and Catholic social thought, 2, 3, 42, 43, 56, 117
exacerbation of wealth inequality by, 18–23, 104–5, 114–15, 120

public policy toward poverty (*cont.*)
  fostering discrimination against
    blacks, 18–22, 87, 101–2, 104–5,
    120
  goals of, 13, 73
  inductive approach to, 76
  need for paradigm shift in, 13, 16,
    103, 109–10
  overemphasis on charity, 55, 119
  to promote savings, 7, 105–7, 122
  See also asset-building policies;
    income-bolstering approach

Quadragesimo Anno (Pius XI), 30–33

Ratzinger, Joseph Cardinal, 154n3
Rawls, John, 62, 67, 68, 73–74
Reconstruction, 88–94
red-lining, 98–99
Rerum Novarum (Leo XIII), 26,
    27–30, 127–28, 137n10, 137n13
restrictive covenants, 97
revelation, divine, 58
rights
  economic, 45–46, 48–50, 72, 86, 123
  human, 70, 73
  natural, 28, 31, 37
  property, 75
Roosevelt, Franklin, 81
Rorty, Richard, 65–66
Rutherford, Stuart, 7

Sampson, Yates, 90
Santorum, Rick, 113
Save the Children, 114
saving and asset accumulation
  in Catholic social thought, 32, 51
  child-based, 110–11
  disincentives for poor, 22–24
  and economic well-being, 13, 57
  and human behavior, 22, 106
  IDAs and, 107–10, 112, 113, 120,
    150n11

need for policies rewarding, 7,
    105–7, 122
  policies favoring nonpoor in, 7, 105
Savings for Working Families Act, 113
Scanlon, Edward, 16
Schram, Sanford, 114
Schreiner, Mark, 79, 82, 103
Schuck, Michael J., 127, 154n2
scripture
  on community, 46–47
  and divine revelation, 58
  on preferential option for poor, 52
Second Vatican Council, 45–46, 49,
    51, 129, 131
sectarianism, 67
segregation, 96–97
Sen, Amartya, 78, 142n1, 143n6
  on human freedom, 83, 134n23
Shapiro, Thomas, 16, 99, 102
sharecropper system, 93
Sherman, William Tecumseh, 92
Sherraden, Margaret, 125
Sherraden, Michael, 129, 131
  on assets as link to future, 82
  on capabilities approach, 63, 142n6
  on child-based asset-building poli-
    cies, 110
  on developing individual capacities,
    5, 83
  on focus and specialization, 78
  on income- vs. asset-based
    approaches, 8, 11, 63
  on inductive approach, 76
  on ownership and political activ-
    ity, 80
  on ownership rights and responsi-
    bilities, 138n22
  on psychosocial effect of assets, 16,
    79, 82
  on regressive nature of asset-based
    policies, 20, 120
  on saving incentives, 23, 103, 107,
    150n11

Shuman, Howard, 21–22
Simon, William E., 142n112
Singapore, 111, 113–14
Smith, Adam, 78–79
social cohesion, 5, 80
social institutions
    capabilities approach to, 74, 124,
        125
    discrimination in, 59, 85, 95–96,
        98–99
    giving poor access to, 22, 57, 107,
        111, 124
    role of in Catholic social thought, 7,
        28–29, 35–36, 44, 45–46, 49, 56
socialism, 27, 31, 137n13
social justice
    capabilities approach to, 61–62, 63,
        125
    in Catholic social thought, 2, 32, 33,
        43, 63, 117, 119, 126
    and toleration of cultural differ-
        ences, 64
social nature of the individual
    in capabilities approach, 71, 124
    in Catholic social thought, 39, 44,
        46–49, 53, 117, 118, 152n54
social networks, 7, 79–80
Social Security, 18, 21, 33–34
    discrimination against African
        Americans in, 95–96
social unrest, 27, 29, 85
Sollicitudo Rei Socialis (John Paul II),
    37
South Africa, 74–75
Southern Homestead Act, 92, 94
South Korea, 111, 113–14
Soviet Union, 36, 139n51
Stiles, Ezra, 81
sweat equity, 78

TANF (Temporary Assistance for
    Needy Families), 108, 150n15
Taparelli d'Azeglio, Luigi, 137n10

taxation policies and deductions, 1
    and poor, 20, 21, 104, 105
    regressive nature of, 18–22
Temporary Assistance for Needy
    Families (TANF), 135n38
Thirteenth Amendment, 89
Troubled Asset Relief Program
    (TARP), 19
Trumbull, Lyman, 92

Uganda, 113–14
Unafraid of the Dark (Bray), 17–18
unemployment, 41–42, 50
United Kingdom, 106, 110, 111,
    113–14
universalism, 143n13
    postmodern critique of, 65–66
Urban Institute, 114
U.S. Catholic Bishops
    1919 statement of, 51
    See also National Conference of
        Catholic Bishops

Valls, Andrew, 101

wages
    Catholic social thought on, 28, 30,
        31–32, 35
    low-wage jobs, 10, 28, 133n14
wealth
    Catholic social thought on, 29, 32,
        35, 36, 38–39, 53, 54–55
    definitions of, 134n24
    excessive concentrations of, 29, 35, 63
    and income, 81
    unequal distribution of, 1, 4, 18–24,
        41, 81–82, 87, 100–101, 103, 149n1
    and well-being, 63, 73–74, 75, 76
wealthy
    Church teachings on, 32, 55, 85
    favored over poor in social policy,
        20, 21, 43
    relationship to poor, 55

wealthy (*cont.*)
  social networks of, 80
  widening gap with poor, 50, 57,
    103, 104
welfare system, 8, 19
  conservatives on, 9–10, 133n16
  and poverty, 17, 24
  PRWORA reform of, 9–12
Women, Infants, and Children food
    program (WIC), 135n38
Women and Human Development
    (Nussbaum), 75–76

Woo, Lillian, 20
workers
  African American, 95, 96
  401(k) plans for, 23, 106
  John XXIII on, 35
  and joint ownership, 31–32, 33, 35,
    51, 138n32
  Leo XIII on, 29, 30, 31–32
  Marxist view of, 74
  Pius XI on, 33
  U.S. bishops on, 42, 51
  See also wages

James P. Bailey is associate professor of theology at Duquesne University.